Organizational Leadership

Organizational Leadership

Sanjay Saxena
Professor and Chairperson
Center for Digital Learning
School of Management Sciences
Varanasi

Purnima Awasthi
Professor
Department of Psychology
Faculty of Social Sciences
Banaras Hindu University
Varanasi

PHI Learning Private Limited
Delhi-110092
2025

*In fond memory of **Shri Asoke K. Ghosh** (October 1942 – February 2024), Founder Chairman and Managing Director of PHI Learning, whose vision endlessly inspires.*

The Legacy Continues....

Published by Pushpita Ghosh, PHI Learning Private Limited, Rimjhim House, 111, Patparganj Industrial Estate, Delhi-110092 and Printed by Syndicate Binders, A-20, Hosiery Complex, Noida, Phase-II Extension, Noida-201305 (N.C.R. Delhi).

₹ 450.00

ORGANIZATIONAL LEADERSHIP
Sanjay Saxena and Purnima Awasthi

ISBN-978-93-5443-814-1 (Print Book)
ISBN-978-93-5443-998-8 (e-Book)

Contents

Preface

Current geoeconomic events indicate significant changes, such as transitioning from a single global reserve currency to a multicurrency basket and shifting from multilateral to bilateral trade agreements. Additionally, the movement of large-scale manufacturing and fintech ventures from the Global West to India suggests that India will emerge as the world's largest manufacturing and financial hub in the next decade. Soon, we will see resident Indians taking on CEO roles at some of the world's leading business organizations based in India. For India to seize this opportunity, all organizations, be they in business, scientific research, education, or government, must strive for excellence in their endeavors. The excellent performance of Indian institutions will position India as a producer of high-quality products and services. Although India has a wealth of world-class human resources with strong technical, engineering, and managerial skills, these individuals often lack leadership competencies for leading organizations toward innovation, excellence, and financial success.

Extensive research has demonstrated that leadership is an observable and learnable phenomenon. It is not a mysterious quality that only a select few can grasp. With the right opportunities, feedback, and practice, individuals with a strong passion and perseverance can improve their leadership skills. A good leader evolves through a continuous process of self-reflection, education, training, experience, creative thinking, and contemplation. This book, "Organizational Leadership," will help you become an incredible leader. It offers advanced insights into leadership concepts and theories, essential attributes and skills, and various functions of leadership. It aims to transform individuals across diverse organizations into exceptional leaders. These leaders are visionary and innovative, and they serve as mentors who possess remarkable abilities to inspire their followers, build self-directed teams, and cultivate a high-performance organizational culture.

This book is organized into 10 chapters. Chapter 1 clarifies key leadership concepts, including the definition of leadership and how it differs from managerial approaches. It explores various leadership perspectives, such as relationship, servant, transactional, transformational, and strategic leadership. Additionally, it discusses different leadership styles and strategies for resolving human conflicts within organizations.

Chapter 2 focuses on various leadership theories that help emerging leaders understand how to synchronize different situations, tasks, bonds between leaders and followers, and their followers' traits, knowledge, skills, competencies, aspirations, and motivations. The text discusses several critical leadership theories, including Action Centered Leadership (ACL), Dunham & Pierce's Leadership Process Model, Fiedler's Contingency Leadership Model, French & Raven's Five Forms of Power, Hersey-Blanchard Situational Leadership Theory, Tannenbaum-Schmidt Leadership Continuum, Path-Goal Theory of Leadership, Leader-Member Exchange Theory (LMX), and Zenger & Folkman's 10 Fatal Leadership Flaws.

Chapter 3 explores the attributes that transform a manager into an integrated leader. It discusses key qualities of a leader, such as proactivity, vision, lateral thinking, resilience, perseverance, and honesty. Additionally, the chapter emphasizes interpersonal skills essential for leadership, including emotional intelligence, effective communication, compassion, and the ability to create synergy.

Chapter 4 explores the primary function of leadership: envisioning and alignment. The content highlights the definitions of envisioning and alignment, the power of a vision, the key characteristics of a compelling vision, the envisioning process, and strategies for emotionally aligning followers with the vision.

Chapter 5 discusses how to lead change in an organization. It highlights the necessity of change, the resistance encountered, strategies leaders can use to overcome this resistance, and the steps involved in the change process.

Chapter 6 teaches readers about mentoring and counseling followers. The text discusses the definitions of mentoring and counseling, the mentor-mentee relationships, and the steps involved in the mentoring and counseling processes.

Chapter 7 focuses on motivation in detail. It emphasizes a conceptual understanding of motivation, discussing need-based and behavioral motivational theories and identifying demotivators and the role of leaders in enhancing motivation. The need-based theories covered in this chapter are Maslow's Hierarchy of Needs, Alderfer's ERG Theory of Motivation, McClelland's Theory of Needs, and Herzberg's Two-Factor Motivation Theory. The key behavioral motivational theories discussed are Goal Setting Theory, Equity Theory, Expectancy Theory, Self-Determination Theory, Csikszentmihalyi's Concept of Flow Experience, and Bandura's Social Cognition Theory.

Chapter 8 focuses on the definition of empowerment and its advantages. It emphasizes the importance of a sense of ownership. It outlines the key differences between employees with a worker's and those with an owner's mindsets. To illustrate the key components of empowerment, this chapter introduces the Bowen and Lawler Empowerment Model and the Spreitzer Psychological Empowerment Model. Additionally, the chapter discusses the main reasons for the failure of empowerment initiatives.

Chapter 9 focuses on building high-performance teams within organizations. It discusses the definition of an effective team, the key differences between a group and a team, the advantages of teamwork, the fundamentals of team dynamics, and the leader's role in developing high-performance teams.

Chapter 10 discusses how to create an effective organizational culture. It outlines the key components and significance of organizational culture, the building blocks of an organizational culture, a high-performance organizational culture, and the VRIO Framework.

We invite readers to share their valuable feedback at phi@phindia.com or sanjay-saxena27@yahoo.com

Sanjay Saxena
Purnima Awasthi

CHAPTER 1

Conceptual Framework of Leadership

Currently, the shift in global wealth from the Global North (U.S., Canada, Britain, and Europe) to the Global South (Asia, Africa, and Latin America) presents numerous opportunities for countries in the Global South to alleviate poverty, improve the quality of life for their people, and take a leadership role in the world. This would not be possible unless various businesses, the government, educational institutions, and scientific research organizations operate at the highest level. One of the main challenges for organizations to operate at their best is cultivating high-performance leadership throughout all levels of the organization. In the current geoeconomic landscape, effective organizational leadership at all levels is crucial for strategically adapting to emerging markets, fostering cross-cultural competence, driving innovation and digital transformation, ensuring sustainable development, and cultivating a skilled workforce in the areas of science, technology, defense, energy, food, and healthcare.

1.1 Organizational Leadership: An Overview

Today, most business organizations, whether public or privately owned, struggle to achieve excellence in their endeavors due to a lack of effective leadership across all hierarchical levels (top, middle, and front levels). As per John Kotter, organizations are overly managed and under-led. This issue is not due to a lack of awareness or knowledge about leadership; rather, it stems from an overemphasis on completing tasks and delivering quick financial results. The owners of business organizations primarily focus on financial outcomes, such as market share, sales revenue, profits, market capitalization, and company valuation. On the other hand, to achieve these financial results, managers at various levels concentrate on ensuring quality production, improving process efficiencies, fostering innovation, multitasking, and accomplishing tasks.

The managers employ a traditional leadership style characterized by a top-down philosophy, where leaders are decisive, efficient, and unemotional, maintaining total control. These managers believe they are effective leaders because they manage tasks well, closely monitor daily operations, manage resources, organize people around management initiatives, and improve operational efficiencies through lean management, benchmarking, cost management, inventory management, or supply chain rationalization.

However, it is crucial to understand that these actions do not define leadership. Suppose we regularly plan, organize, control, and execute all operations efficiently. In that case, we may think we are displaying outstanding leadership skills. Nonetheless, the truth is that we are merely excelling at managerial duties and not necessarily demonstrating leadership qualities.

Before addressing questions like "What is leadership?" or "What are the various functions of leadership?", we want to highlight a research study that examines the consequences of placing too much emphasis on managerial practices to achieve bottom-line results while neglecting effective leadership practices within the organization.

In Figure 1.1, the vertical axis represents managerial practices, ranging from low to high, while the horizontal axis represents leadership practices, also moving from low to high. Research outcomes have shown that organizations with high managerial practices but low emphasis on leadership tend to create a phobic environment, which results in low psychological energy, average performance, high employee turnover, significant conflicts, and, in extreme scenarios, legal cases. Organizations with high leadership practices but low emphasis on managerial practices tend to create an environment resembling a recreation club with little challenge, minimal effort, empty talk, and average performance.

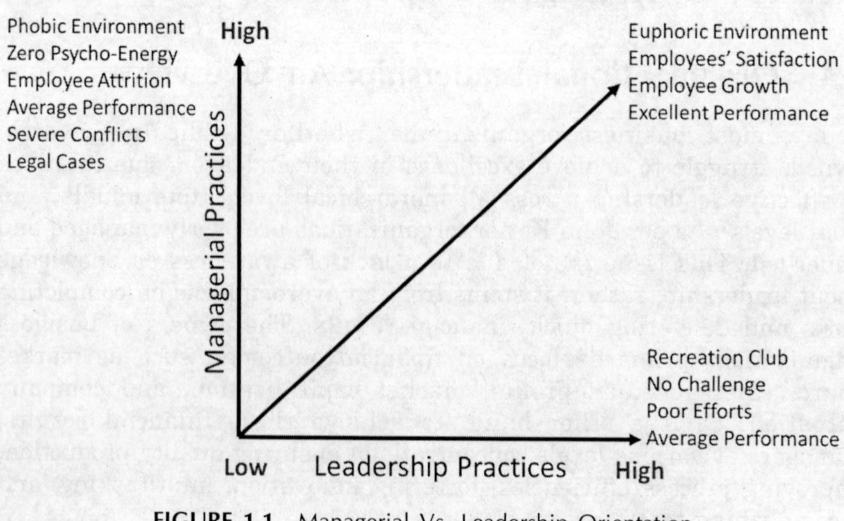

FIGURE 1.1 Managerial Vs. Leadership Orientation.

Therefore, it is clear that to build a high-performance organization, we must equally focus on effective leadership and management practices. Excellent managerial practices stabilize the organization and execute all decisions to generate productive results.

However, sustaining profitability, productivity, quality, and good customer service is challenging without effective leadership in private and public organizations. In dozens of different ways, researchers have demonstrated that leadership does make a difference. In various organizations, top management and other stakeholders believe that the organization cannot remain competitive without effective leadership.

What is Leadership?

Many managers make the mistake of comparing individuals in the organization to other resources such as machines, materials, or money. People are not robots designed to work without desires, aspirations, and expectations. People have different degrees of desires, emotions, aspirations, and expectations. As a result, we cannot manage human beings as we do with materials, money, or machines; instead, we can only guide and lead them. It is the leadership role to guide and lead people in the right direction. Therefore, we typically say: "Manage things, Lead people."

Effective leadership provides a signature experience for its subordinates by elevating their vision to greater heights and enhancing their personalities beyond usual limitations. Employees get a signature experience when they have ample opportunities to perform, receive proper mentoring for personal and professional growth, become their best expression, and reach extraordinary heights in their careers. They enjoy this signature experience when they feel happy, joyful, and energized, working in a high-performance culture alongside wonderful colleagues.

Leaders act as change agents, driving transformations in individuals, processes, and organizational environments. In contrast to managers who operate within the organizational paradigm, leaders navigate between that paradigm and guide the organization and its people to uncharted territories, creating an entirely new organizational paradigm.

Leaders use their envisioning skills to create a vision representing the organization's future. They emotionally align people with their vision and motivate them to take the initiative to achieve it. They serve as mentors, identifying and nurturing their subordinates' hidden potential through effective mentoring, coaching, and teaching. Leaders cultivate a motivating climate to achieve outstanding organizational success, empower their subordinates to take ownership of tasks, develop self-directed teams, and build a high-performance organizational culture.

1.2 Leadership Approaches Vs. Managerial Approaches

Today, most organizations are under-led and over-managed. Leadership must be developed in organizations because the people in charge are too concerned with keeping things on time and budget and with doing what was done yesterday, only doing it better (John P. Kotter, 1990).

As illustrated in Figure 1.2, today's organizations face a significant challenge. While many individuals are involved in management, only a few take on leadership roles, and even fewer possess the integrated skills and qualities needed to tackle leadership and management challenges effectively.

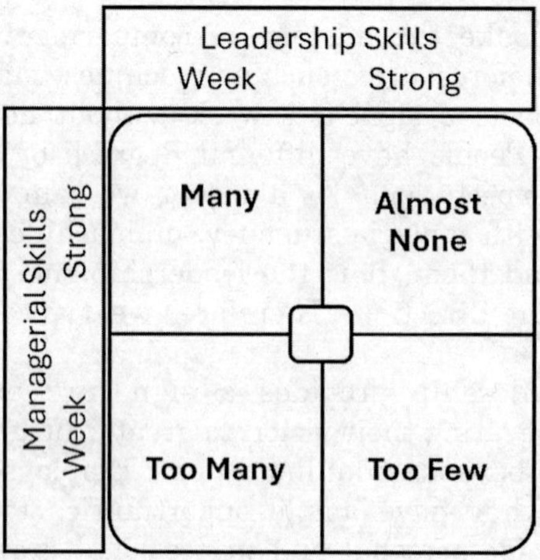

FIGURE 1.2 Leader Manager Grid.

Organizations that are satisfied with mediocrity can manage only with managerial approaches. However, those who seek to stand out and achieve excellence need strong leadership. Truly outstanding companies accomplish this through passionate leadership. In our highly competitive era of globalization, where businesses strive to develop capabilities surpassing their rivals, effective leadership at all levels is crucial for achieving these objectives.

An organization with individuals possessing strong leadership and managerial skills can achieve greater robustness and pose significant challenges for competitors to replicate its competencies. There is tremendous demand for world-class leader-managers who know when to lead and when to manage. Leaders guide people and foster a positive work culture to drive excellence in all organizational performance. At the same time, managers handle processes, plan activities, and organize and control to stabilize the environment and enhance productivity. One of the primary responsibilities of a leader is to develop people and enable them to reach their full potential.

The earlier discussion highlights that managers primarily focus on achieving bottom-line results through planning, organizing, and controlling tasks and processes. In contrast, leaders concentrate on people's development and motivation. The bottom-line results include revenue, profits, and market capitalization. The development and motivation of individuals focuses on enhancing their skills, knowledge, and competencies, as well as administering their personal and professional growth, happiness, and well-being. Ultimately, both the managerial and leadership approaches help achieve the organizational vision envisioned by the leaders. It is clear that leadership and managerial practices differ significantly; however, they complement each other regarding final organizational outcomes.

Leaders and managers are not distinct individuals; once companies understand the fundamental differences between leadership and management, they groom their managers to provide both.

Figure 1.3 illustrates two distinct yet complementary approaches to leadership and management.

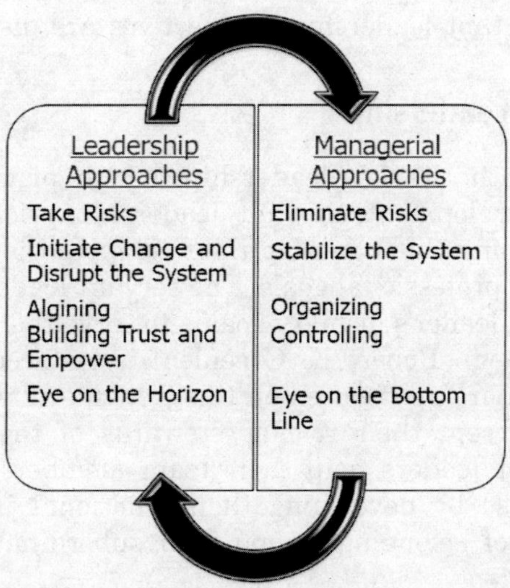

FIGURE 1.3 Managerial Approaches Vs. Leadership Approaches.

Leaders see the organization not just as it is today but as what it has the potential to become. They focus on the horizon and operate between paradigms. They take risks by challenging the status quo, initiating changes, and disrupting existing systems. Managers focus on stabilizing systems by eliminating risks and generating bottom-line performance through efficient management of materials and tasks. Effective leaders serve as change agents, constantly looking toward the future to elevate their organizations to new heights, and that is why they keep their eyes on the horizon. In contrast, managers act as stabilizers, focusing on optimizing systems to enhance productivity. They concentrate on the organization's bottom-line performance.

Leaders focus on aligning people emotionally with the change process and winning their commitment rather than organizing them around it. Rather than implementing control systems, leaders emphasize building trust and empowering their subordinates to foster a sense of ownership. They encourage their team members to take initiative and make decisions.

Managers facilitate change initiatives to keep projects on track by organizing organizational resources, including materials, equipment, and financial resources. They implement control systems, such as tasks, deadlines, policies, rules, and regulations, to manage the entire process.

1.3 Leadership Perspectives

Leadership can be viewed from different perspectives, offering unique insights into the actions of leaders and the methods they use to achieve their goals. Important leadership perspectives are discussed below:

1.3.1 Servant Leadership

In contrast to authoritarian leadership, which primarily focuses on organizational development, servant leadership prioritizes the needs of employees, helping them develop their competencies while achieving both personal and professional goals. The servant leadership perspective emphasizes that a leader's primary goal is to serve their followers rather than dominate them. Robert K. Greenleaf introduced this concept in 1970. Servant leaders are focused on the growth and well-being of their followers. They accept their role as stewards of their organizational resources. Servant leaders help their team members resolve conflicts and manage stress by developing their emotional intelligence. They cultivate a sense of belonging among their subordinates.

1.3.2 Relationship Perspective

Joseph Rost from the University of San Diego is recognized for his 1991 work, which highlights the transition from the traditional, leader-centered view of leadership to what he terms the post-industrial concept of leadership. In his book, *Leadership for the Twenty-First Century*, Rost presents a definition grounded in this post-industrial perspective, which he argues is more aligned with the realities of modern organizational life. His definition describes leadership as an influential relationship between leaders and followers that aims to achieve genuine changes that reflect their shared purposes.

This contemporary definition is composed of four basic components, each of which is essential and must be present if a particular relationship is to be called leadership:

1. **Influence:** The relationship is centered on influence, which is a multidirectional phenomenon. It can flow in any direction and is not limited to a top-down approach. Additionally, attempts to influence must not be coercive. As a result, this relationship relies on persuasion rather than authority.
2. **Everyone's Involvement:** Leaders and followers are the key individuals in this relationship. If we define leadership as a relational process, then both leaders and followers engage in acts of leadership. While not all participants in this dynamic are equal, it can be said that all active participants exert influence. Typically, there are multiple followers and several leaders involved in this arrangement.
3. **Genuine Changes:** Leaders and followers aim for significant changes. "Aim" indicates that leaders and followers actively promote and seek these changes. "Significant" means that the changes desired by leaders and followers must be substantial.
4. **Mutual Purposes:** The changes that leaders and followers seek should reflect their shared goals. These desired changes must consider both the leader's wishes and the followers' desires (Rost, 1991).

Rost reminds us that leadership is not solely defined by what leaders do. Instead, leadership is a shared responsibility between leaders and followers aimed at the collective good. In today's society, leaders operate within a collaborative environment alongside followers. A single leader no longer possesses all the answers or the sole authority to instigate significant change. Instead, we now inhabit a world where many individuals engage in leadership, some as leaders and others as followers. Only by working together can we achieve successful changes for our common purposes.

Many organizational theorists would agree that Rost's definition is more consistent with the type of leadership needed in contemporary society. Slowly, scholars and practitioners alike are abandoning the traditional leadership approaches rooted in the industrial paradigm. Therefore, the essence of leadership is not the leader but the relationship.

1.3.3 Transactional Leadership

Transactional leadership emphasizes the extrinsic relationship between leaders and followers. It examines the mutual benefits of an exchange-based relationship, where the leader offers certain things, such as resources or rewards, in return for others, including the followers' commitment or acceptance of the leader's authority. This type of leadership is best suited for situations where consistency and routine are critical.

Transactional leaders guide or motivate their followers toward established goals by clarifying role and task requirements. In fine, we can say that transactional leaders:

- Enable ordinary people to perform routine tasks effectively.
- Clarify the business's needs and break them down into manageable objectives.
- Evaluate staff needs and reward them accordingly.
- Very effective for improving and maintaining performance.
- Determine the abilities of staff and delegate the job accordingly.

1.3.4 Transformational Leadership

A transformational leader inspires people to take action, transforming followers into leaders and potentially inspiring them to become agents of change. Such leaders empower others to bring their intentions to life and maintain that momentum. Their approach involves pulling rather than pushing; they motivate through shared identity rather than by using rewards or punishments. Leadership is a responsibility, and the effectiveness of this role is evident in the attitudes of those being led.

In the twenty-first century, transformational leaders are those who stay ahead of the change curve. They constantly redefine their industries, create new markets, blaze new trails, reinvent competitive rules, and challenge the status quo. These leaders achieve their goals by looking ahead, scanning the landscape, observing the competition, identifying emerging trends, and discovering new opportunities while avoiding potential crises. They possess a clear vision, a strong passion, and an inspiring aspiration. They unleash tremendous psychological energy by sharing their vision with everyone in the organization. This energy fuels the organization, enabling it to outpace its competitors.

Transformational leaders play a crucial role in developing their followers into leaders by modeling, mentoring, teaching, and empowering them. They help boost their followers' self-esteem and begin by creating a vision that unites a diverse group of people within the organization. This vision serves as a tool to inspire and provide a common direction for everyone.

These leaders guide individuals from a stage of denial to one of commitment, empowering them to take initiative and make decisions. They actively encourage employees to participate in developing the organizational mission, ensuring that each employee feels a sense of ownership and stake in that mission.

Transformational leaders focus on each employee's individual needs for growth and development. They intrinsically motivate and inspire their team members, recognize their performances, offer rewards, and celebrate small victories. They encourage people to exceed expectations and advocate for going the extra mile.

Four Powers of Transformational Leaders

As shown in Figure 1.4, the four powers of transformational leaders are Presence, Intention, Wisdom, and Compassion.

1. **Presence:** Transformational leaders are always present in the environment, much like the aroma of delicious food, the tranquility of monasteries, and the scent of incense sticks. Their ambitions, aspirations, and vision continuously inspire and energize the people within the organization. They diligently embrace their roles as mentors and stewards, caring for everyone involved in the organization.
2. **Intention:** Their intentions are noble as they perform their duties selflessly. They are dedicated to sacrificing for others, focused on achieving organizational goals, loyal to their colleagues, committed to their ethical standards, and aligned with the organization's core values. They create trust and a sense of belonging within their team while demonstrating integrity and a strong work ethic. They challenge the status quo and seek to transform the organization for long-term success. They aim to cultivate a high-performance culture to ensure that employees have a signature experience while working in the organization.
3. **Wisdom:** Their wisdom enables them to maintain balance, manage emotions, and effectively apply their knowledge and skills for organizational development. They stay composed in challenging situations and use their wisdom to explore all available options before making decisions. Their choices are always aimed at benefiting the greater good. They understand

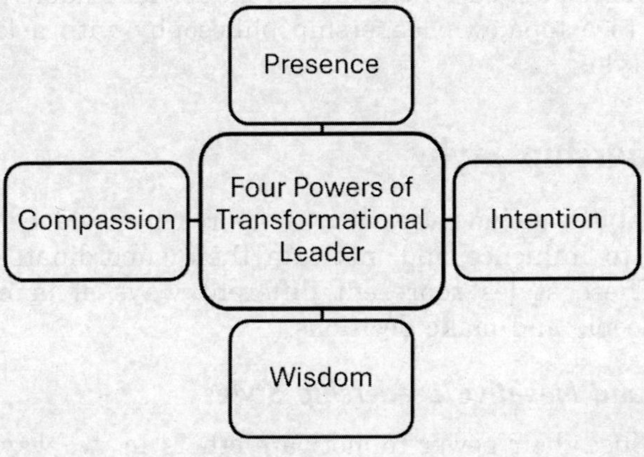

FIGURE 1.4 Four Powers of a Transformational Leader.

that leadership is not about exerting control; instead, it is about empowering others to succeed.

4. **Compassion:** Compassionate leaders empathize with their subordinates to understand their emotions and challenges, showing a willingness to help them overcome problems or limitations. They are enthusiastic, creative, and spontaneous, occasionally using their intellect but consistently following their hearts.

Satya Nadella's Transformational Leadership at Microsoft

Satya Nadella became the CEO of Microsoft in 2014. At the time of his appointment, Microsoft was struggling with a lack of innovation, low employee morale, and a rigid culture. When Satya took over, he implemented several transformational actions:

- He emphasizes inclusivity and openness in the organizational climate, ensuring employees feel valued and motivated.
- He shifted Microsoft's culture from a competitive, know-it-all environment to a collaborative, learn-it-all culture, fostering innovation and creativity.
- He inspired employees with a clear and compelling vision, modeling behavior, mentoring them, and empowering them to innovate.
- He pivoted Microsoft towards cloud computing, artificial intelligence, and subscription-based services like Office 365, making the company more agile and future-oriented.

Under Satya's exceptional transformational leadership, Microsoft's market value rose significantly from $300 billion in 2014 to $2.5 trillion in 2024. His leadership has made Microsoft one of the most valuable and innovative companies globally. Microsoft's immense financial success over the past decade is a prime example of the importance of transformational leadership. It serves as the best answer for all current managers who remain entrenched in the industrial leadership paradigm and adhere to a top-down leadership philosophy with a transactional leadership style.

1.4 Leadership Styles

Leadership styles include the various approaches and behaviors that leaders use to influence and motivate their subordinates and make decisions. These styles represent different ways of using power to encourage people and make decisions.

1. *Positive and Negative Leadership Styles*

Leaders can use their power to motivate others in two ways: positively and negatively. Using power positively to inspire others is a positive leadership style, while the opposite is true for negative power usage.

As illustrated in Figure 1.5, a positive leadership style involves publicly recognizing and praising employees' contributions, providing monetary rewards, enhancing job security, and delegating additional responsibilities. This leadership style promotes employee development by increasing job satisfaction, improving productivity, reducing employee turnover, fostering innovation and creativity, and building a high-performance organizational culture. In contrast, the negative leadership style encompasses creating a fearful environment through threats, coercion, fines, suspensions, and, in extreme cases, termination of employees. The negative leadership style significantly lowers employee happiness and well-being and increases employee turnover. Where there are threats and coercion, innovation, creativity, and happiness vanish. They cannot coexist; one must be eradicated.

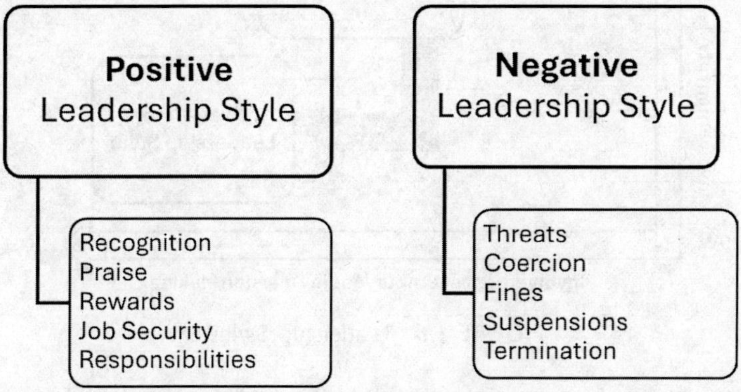

FIGURE 1.5 Positive and Negative Leadership Styles.

Kalanick's Negative Leadership Style at Uber

Travis Kalanick was the co-founder and CEO of Uber from 2010 to 2017. As soon as he took over as CEO, he began cultivating a toxic culture by fostering cutthroat competition among Uber employees, which in turn encouraged aggression, workplace harassment, discrimination, and unethical practices. Finally, due to mounting pressure from public reports about the company's unethical corporate culture, including the disregard for workplace harassment, Kalanick resigned from Uber in 2017.

2. *Decision-Making Style*

Effective and timely decision-making is essential for business success, and leaders bear the primary responsibility. They must also involve employees in the decision-making process. Regarding employees' involvement—whether complete, partial, or none—in the decision-making process, leaders adopt various approaches that can be categorized into three basic types of leadership styles: autocratic, participative, and free-rein. Figure 1.6 illustrates autocratic, participative, and free-rein leadership styles based on the levels of involvement of leaders and employees in the decision-making process.

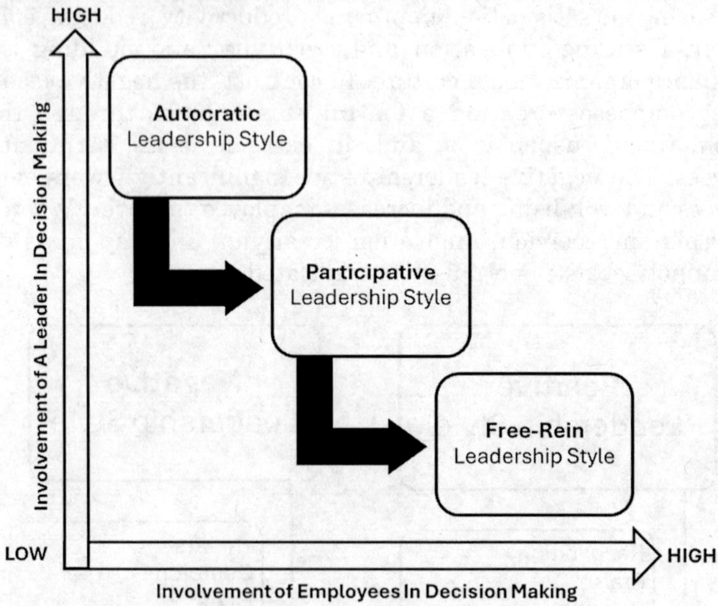

FIGURE 1.6 Leadership Styles.

(a) Autocratic Leadership Style: In autocratic decision-making, the leader's involvement in the process is significantly high, while the participation of employees is minimal. The leader makes decisions independently, with little to no flexibility for employee involvement. In this style, leaders use their authority and do not seek input from subordinates. The leader makes decisions and expects subordinates to comply with them. In other words, they impose their decisions and initiatives on the employees.

The autocratic decision-making style is preferred when employees lack experience or knowledge, when pressure arises, or when trust between leaders and followers is lacking. It is effective in crises; however, consistently using this approach can lead to decreased employee morale, diminished creativity and innovation, and, in severe cases, increased employee turnover.

Kodak's Failure under Autocratic Leadership

George Fisher served as Kodak's CEO from 1993 to 1999. When Fisher took over, Kodak was a dominant player in the photography industry and held a monopoly in the sales of film and film cameras. He was an autocratic leader who took strict control over decision-making and denied the participation of frontline employees. He discouraged risk-taking behavior in the organization and created a rigid corporate culture.

Kodak invented the digital camera in 1975, but Fisher and previous CEOs ignored digital innovation because they feared losing film sales. Employees advocating for digital innovation were sidelined. Meanwhile, competitors like Sony, Canon, and Nikon rapidly embraced digital photography. As a result, by the early 2000s, Kodak lost its dominance in the photography industry and ultimately filed for bankruptcy in 2012. Kodak's case clearly illustrates how risky it is to overlook employees' involvement in the strategic decision-making process.

(b) Participative Leadership Style: This style is characterized by leaders involving subordinates in decisions. Leaders who follow this style believe in "no involvement, no commitment." The leader has final authority over decisions in the participative decision-making process. Still, employees are encouraged to share their opinions and suggestions. Emphasis is placed on open discussions to address problems, and a leader acts as a guide and facilitator. The participative leadership style embraces greater commitment from employees and enhances their sense of ownership, creativity, morale, and job satisfaction. However, this democratic process is time-consuming and sometimes leads to conflicts among employees due to disagreements.

Toyota's Success under Participative Leadership

When Toyota faced quality control issues in its car manufacturing, the company introduced the Toyota Production System (TPS), which includes continuous improvement (Kaizen) and quality circles. Employees at all levels were encouraged to identify problems and suggest solutions, empowering them to implement these solutions and rewarding them for solving genuine issues. This participative approach improved production efficiency, reduced waste, and enhanced product quality. As a result, Toyota became one of the leading automobile manufacturers in the world.

(c) Free-Rein Leadership Style: The free-rein leadership style encourages individuals or groups to function independently. The leader sets limits, allows followers to resolve problems, or empowers individuals to set goals. This style relies on the leaders' trust in their employees' skills and self-motivation.

The free-rein leadership style necessitates considerable groundwork to align individuals with the organization's vision, mission, and goals and develop their knowledge, skills, and competencies through effective mentoring. Managers who lack the time and patience to invest in this foundational work revert to an autocratic leadership style or implement a participative style in a dictatorial manner.

1.5 Resolving Human Conflicts within the Organization

Leaders play a vital role in resolving conflicts within organizations. Conflicts among individuals are a natural occurrence in any workplace. However, if these conflicts go unresolved, they can lead to serious adverse outcomes, including increased employee turnover, lawsuits, absenteeism, workplace violence, poor decision-making, and harmful effects on both the physical and mental health of employees. Recent research shows that leaders spend about 90 percent of their time resolving conflicts within their organizations.

Conflict occurs when one person or group feels that another person or group is negatively judging or undermining their efforts. Interpersonal or intergroup conflicts can manifest in three ways: disagreements over goals, strained relationships between individuals or groups, and differing opinions on accomplishing tasks.

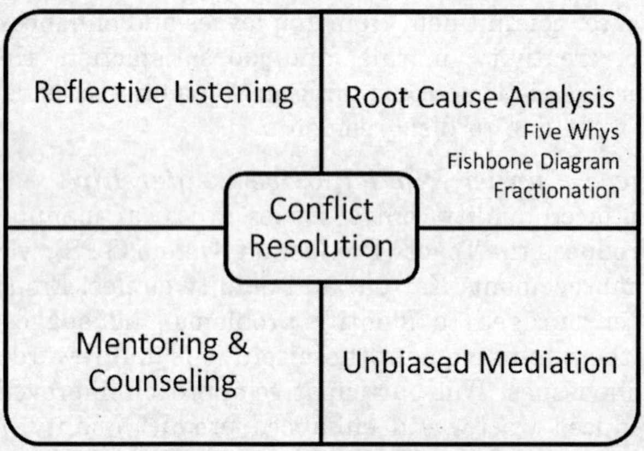

FIGURE 1.7 Steps in Resolving Conflicts.

It is the acumen of a leader to understand the root causes of conflict and solve them with an unbiased approach. As shown in Figure 1.7, there are some essential steps a leader should embrace to resolve conflicts more effectively:

1. Listen Reflectively: Reflective listening is widely used in therapeutic purposes such as counseling, conflict resolution, and interpersonal persuasion. In reflective listening, a leader actively listens to people involved in conflict by mirroring their spoken words, thoughts, and emotions. During the mirroring process, a leader restates what an individual or group has expressed. This indicates that the listener understands the meaning accurately. Leaders improve their understanding of emotions by identifying and articulating the underlying feelings of speakers. To ensure an accurate understanding of conflicts,

leaders clarify issues by asking questions from speakers. During the process of reflective listening, leaders remain non-judgmental by staying open, avoiding criticism, and not offering spontaneous advice.

The questions asked during reflective listening generally aim to gain clarity, encourage further sharing, understand others' feelings, explore perspectives, and summarize key points. Here are some examples of questions that can be used in reflective listening:

- What do you mean when you say it is impossible to work here?
- Can you help me understand this better?
- What happened next?
- Can you tell me more about that?
- I can understand how you are feeling in this situation. Are you depressed?
- What do you think could help in this situation?
- It sounds like you are feeling depressed because of poor interpersonal relationships with your immediate boss. Is that right?

2. Identify the Root Cause through Root Cause Analysis: Root Cause Analysis (RCA) is a systematic process that identifies the underlying cause of a problem. In every conflict situation, the issues that are visible on the surface are often just symptoms of a deeper problem. Addressing only these symptoms may not resolve the conflict and can even make the situation worse. For instance, consider a meeting where Ms. Sara and Mr. Johar are arguing intensely. A leader might mistakenly interpret this situation as a sign of poor interpersonal relationships between the two. However, if we explore the conflict more deeply, we may discover that the argument stems from a lack of clarity in their job roles and significant overlap in their responsibilities. It may not resolve the underlying issues if we use our authority to request that they do not argue during the meeting and maintain a professional demeanor. However, if we redefine and clarify their job roles, the tension between them will likely dissipate, leading to improved collaboration.

Therefore, once all the information is collected and a clear understanding of conflicts and underlying emotions is developed, it is time to analyze the facts and find the root cause of the conflict. The root causes of conflicts can include poor communication, miscommunication, misalignment with goals, lack of consensus on procedures, unequal resource allocation, breakdown in unity of command, unclear job roles, and strained interpersonal relationships.

Essential Techniques for Conducting Root Cause Analysis

Various techniques are used in conducting root cause analysis; however, two important ones are explained here:

(a) **Five Whys:** The 'five whys' is a common technique used to find the root cause of any problem. In this technique, the investigator repeatedly asks "why" five times to drill down into the root cause of a specific issue. The following is an example of identifying the root cause:

Problem Statement: Suresh and Elina, two employees, frequently argue in team meetings, which disrupts teamwork.

- *Why are Suresh and Elina arguing?*
  They disagree on project priorities.
- *Why do they disagree on priorities?*
  Suresh prioritizes customer satisfaction, while Elina emphasizes efficiency and cost reduction.
- *Why does Suresh focus on customer satisfaction while Elina focuses on efficiency and cost reduction?*
  Suresh works in customer service, and Elina works in finance.
- *Why do their roles create conflicting priorities?*
  Project planning has no precise alignment between customer needs and budget constraints.
- *Why is there no precise alignment?*
  The company lacks a structured process to balance customer satisfaction with financial efficiency in decision-making.

Root Cause: Lack of a structured process to align various priorities.

Solution: Initiate a discussion across departments to identify a balanced solution.

(b) **Fishbone Diagram (Ishikawa Diagram):** A Fishbone Diagram, also called an Ishikawa Diagram or Cause-and-Effect Diagram, is a visual tool that systematically identifies and presents the potential causes of a specific problem. To create a fishbone diagram, follow these steps:

- Clearly mention the issue at the top of the fishbone. This heading represents the issue we aim to analyze.
- Draw a horizontal arrow that points to the problem statement. This arrow serves as the "spine" of the fish.
- Draw multiple major branches downward from the horizontal arrow to represent the categories of potential causes identified during data coding.
- Analyze all identified categories and create subthemes for each one.

An example of root cause analysis using a fishbone diagram is shown in Figure 1.8.

Problem Statement: Devashish, the Project Manager, and Rahul, the Developer, are experiencing an interpersonal problem, causing communication breakdowns and missed deadlines.

Main Categories of Causes: As shown in the fishbone diagram (Figure 1.8), four main categories may be causing the interpersonal conflicts between Devashish and Rahul. These categories are Communication Issues, Workload and Responsibilities, Personality Differences, Expectations, and End Results.

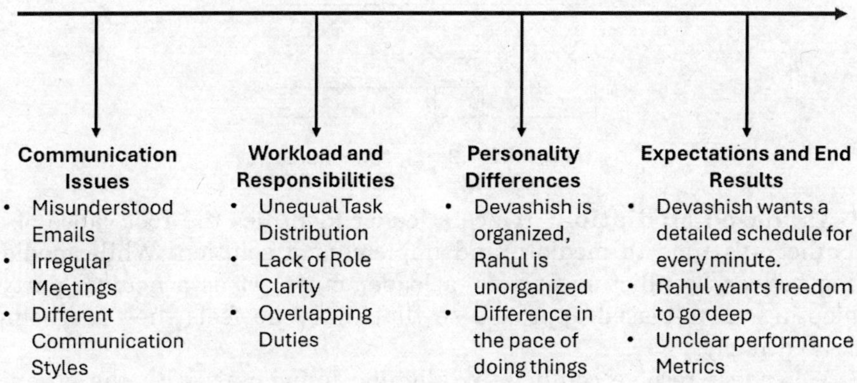

FIGURE 1.8 Fishbone Diagram.

Besides, the fishbone diagram illustrates potential causes within each category identified through brainstorming. Further investigations found the two leading causes of interpersonal conflict between Devashish and Rahul, which are mentioned below:

- Rahul feels tense due to Devashish's micromanagement.
- There are irregular meetings between Devashish and Rahul.

Solution

- Establish clear performance metrics and instruct Devashish not to micromanage while empowering Rahul to complete the task within deadlines.
- Structure compulsory formal weekly meetings between Devashish and the developers.

(c) **Fractionation:** The steps involved in this technique are as follows:

- As shown in Figure 1.9, a group of participants is asked to divide a problem into two units or fractions. These fractions are further divided into two more fractions, and so on, until a satisfactory number of fractions is obtained.
- The fraction lists obtained above are given to another group of participants. They are asked to reassemble them to generate a new perspective on the situation.
- Once the new perspectives are generated, leaders can identify the real problem and begin seeking solutions.

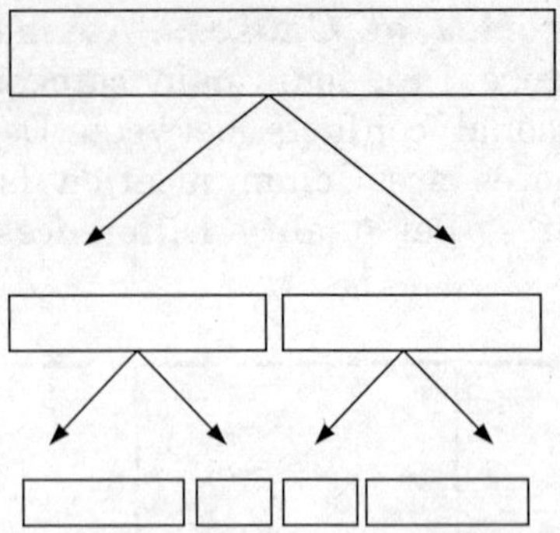

FIGURE 1.9 Fractionation.

3. Unbiased Mediation: Once a leader identifies the root cause of a conflict, it's time to mediate and implement a solution. While mediating between conflicting parties, a leader must act as a neutral party, adopting an unbiased approach so that everyone feels they are being treated fairly.

Leaders resolve conflicts by aligning individuals with the organization's values, norms, vision, goals, and strategies, eliminating misunderstandings, reestablishing unity of commands and reporting relationships, and building consensus around a common approach to work. Also, they create an environment of trust and facilitate smooth communication between individuals or groups.

Satya Nadella's Approach to Mediation for Conflict Resolution at Microsoft

When Satya Nadella became CEO of Microsoft in 2014, he discovered that there were tensions between the Windows and Azure teams. The leaders of both divisions are constantly clashing, which causes inefficiencies and delays in innovation. Nadella identified the root causes of these tensions as the issue of leadership authority over both teams and a mindset of working in silos. He adopted the following mediation approach:

- **Listening to Both Teams:** Nadella personally met both leaders to hear their perspectives, frustrations, and mindsets.
- **Common Ground:** He helped both leaders change their mindsets to see 'One Microsoft' instead of siloed departments working individually, and to think of collaboration instead of compromise.
- **Reassessing Roles:** Nadella reshuffled leadership positions by changing the organizational structure and assigning formal authority to enhance cooperation.

Nadella's mediation enhanced teamwork among departments, fostered innovation, streamlined product development, and successfully guided Microsoft's shift toward cloud computing. This shift was one of the primary reasons for the substantial increase in the company's value.

4. Mentoring and Counseling: Merely solving conflicts will not effectively resolve the underlying issues between individuals or groups. It necessitates thorough follow-up backed by effective mentoring and counseling efforts.

Leaders must be trained to offer mentoring and counseling to their subordinates. Research shows that most organizational conflicts (related to goals, relationships, or action plans) arise from perceptual distortions and inadequate behavioral skills among individuals. Many individuals have a negative outlook on work and others, shaped by past negative experiences, self-centered behavior, and poor interpersonal skills.

Leaders' mentoring and counseling efforts assist individuals in overcoming these behavioral obstacles. The mentoring requirement extends beyond addressing behavioral issues; it also aims to instill the organization's values, norms, and vision in individuals, helping them understand the importance of organizational hierarchies, unity of command, teamwork, and effective communication. Great leaders can prevent most organizational conflicts by developing employees through mentoring and counseling.

1.6 Strategic Leadership

Another leadership perspective is strategic leadership, in which the leaders perform their role as organizational builders with a visionary and strategic approach. As shown in Figure 1.10, the strategic leaders work between the paradigms. They are responsible for a paradigm shift in the organization. They are visionaries with exceptional skills in looking beyond the horizon, seeing the invisible, scanning their organizations and external environments as a whole from a helicopter view, and transforming the ordinary organization into an extraordinary one.

FIGURE 1.10 Strategic Leadership.

Overall, strategic leadership involves guiding the entire organization through highly competitive, complex, and dynamic environments to achieve organizational success. Strategic leaders influence employees to realize the organization's vision, mission, and long-term goals. They collaborate with various teams within the organization, empower them, and encourage innovation at all levels. Additionally, they strive to balance the interests of different groups associated with the organization.

Strategic leaders act as change agents by initiating organization-wide transformations to improve overall effectiveness. They begin by envisioning a clear future, then take risks to disrupt the organization's existing systems, processes, and culture. Following this disruption, they develop strategies to realign these elements with the world's current requirements. When systems are disrupted, people will likely resist these changes for various reasons. Leaders must communicate effectively to address employees' resistance and align them with the change process. This involves ensuring that the purpose, benefits, and processes of the change are clearly understood.

1.6.1 Strategic Leadership Cycle

There is no finishing line for leadership and organizational development. The best leaders are constantly preparing for tomorrow. The environment changes every moment, so today's success becomes tomorrow's status quo. Similarly, new business portfolios that are profitable in the present and considered as factors for organizational growth may become boons to organizations in the future and contribute intensively to making the organizations overweight.

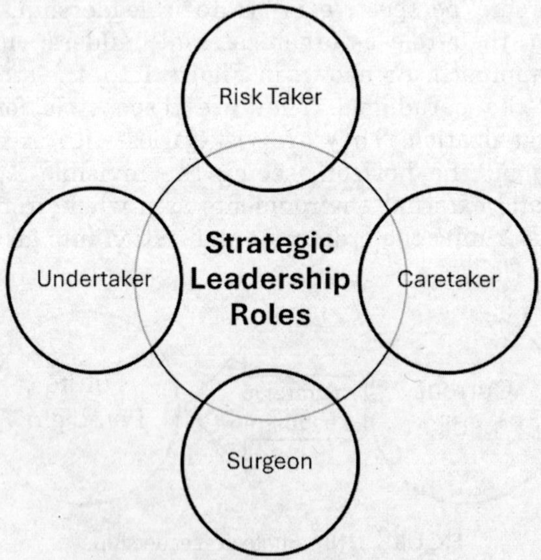

FIGURE 1.11 Strategic Leadership Roles.

Figure 1.11 shows four strategic leadership roles that must be performed at different stages of organizational development in this constantly changing environment: risk-taker, caretaker, surgeon, and undertaker (Rothschild, 1993).

As risk-takers, we must be visionary, missionary, and innovators. We need to develop the organization based on our own dreams. This involves exploring various systems within the organization and assessing their effectiveness in the broader environment by looking around ourselves and beyond the immediate horizons. Through this analysis and our intuitive skills, we can introduce different portfolios that will drive growth for our organization.

Once the organization starts sailing on a new path and direction with various portfolios, we can switch to our caretaker role to institutionalize the system so that the company grows profitably, perhaps for decades. The caretaker works within the organizational paradigm and creates order to increase productivity with the help of proper planning, organizing, directing, and controlling functions. Different businesses can be productive for various periods depending on the Industry and product life cycles.

When the business becomes overweight, complacent, and slow, and some portfolios burden the organization, it is time for the surgeon to take command. Surgeon leaders are analytical, objective, and free from the past—nothing is sacred to them. They focus on the vital organs of the business and determine the most profitable way to remove the organs that lack strategic fit. They perform skilled surgery to remove those organs.

After a successful surgery, we need to organize to work as a shock absorber against the surgical effects and concentrate on future business development. Much patience is required to absorb these shocks.

Steve Jobs's Strategic Leadership in Apple's Turnaround

In 1997, Apple Computer Inc. was on the brink of bankruptcy, and its CEO, Gil Amelio, was ousted after 12 years of poor performance. Michael Dell, the founder, chairman, and CEO of Dell Technologies, famously stated that if he were in charge of Apple, he would have shut it down and returned the shareholders' money. However, Steve Jobs had a different vision when he rejoined Apple in July 1997 as interim CEO.

Steve Jobs' return to Apple marked the beginning of the company's turnaround. Between 1997 and 2010, he made several strategic decisions that helped pull Apple out of bankruptcy, transforming it into a technology titan. In 2006, Apple surpassed Dell in market capitalization. Each product released by Apple became synonymous with success. By October 2010, Apple's stock price had soared from $6 per share in 1997 to $300 per share. Here are some of the major strategic decisions made by Jobs during this transformative period:

1. **Creative Partnership:** As a risk-taker in 1997, Steve Jobs formed a partnership with Microsoft, announcing a five-year

contract to produce Mac computers equipped with Microsoft Office. Microsoft agreed to invest $150 million in Apple. In 2006, Apple struck a deal with Intel to utilize its Core Duo chip technology in the MacBook Pro and iMac, significantly enhancing their performance. Jobs acquired Macromedia's Final Cut product to expand further into the software arena.

2. **Discard the Project:** Jobs abandoned the Newton Project as a surgeon, which had consumed $100 million from a struggling company. He also abruptly halted the Macintosh Licensing Program.
3. **Discontinued Products:** Again, as a surgeon, Steve reduced Apple's 15 product lines to four products in the desktop and Macintosh categories. For the first time, Apple was notably lean and streamlined in the number of products offered.
4. **Repositioning:** After the surgery of projects and products, Apple Inc. was quite vulnerable and lean, requiring someone to take on the role of undertaker. As an undertaker, Steve Jobs' other main concern was changing Apple's unhealthy, damaged image. Through "Think Different" ads and catchy slogans, Apple positioned the Macintosh as a stylish alternative to its competitors' computer brands. In 2007, Jobs changed the company's name from Apple Computer Inc. to Apple Inc. This was done to communicate to the world that Apple is no longer limited to just manufacturing computers. It aims to produce other tech products that will change people's lives.
5. **Cultural Shift:** Steve Jobs understood the significance of transforming the company's work culture to engage every employee in a performance mode. He conveyed to employees that he meant business and began rejecting hundreds of their ideas related to process improvement, product enhancement, or new product development. He believed that accomplishing something deemed impossible generates higher motivation in us, as we have the experience to share with our children that we were a part of an extraordinary project.

   Jobs also valued strict routines of secrecy. At Apple, he implemented a "closed-door policy" that permitted employees to access only their assigned areas. New hires were placed in dummy roles until they earned trust. He championed organizational values like simplicity, differentiation, creating experiences, making tough decisions, taking risks, and delivering excellent products in improved packaging.
6. **Distribution Channels:** In his role as an undertaker, Jobs launched Apple's website for the first time in 1998 to sell its products directly to consumers. On May 15, 2001, Apple opened its Apple Store, which was a brilliant idea. Apple aimed to provide its products with the proper shelf life and space, which

other retailers were not offering. Through Apple Stores, the company created a genuine consumer experience in the stores.

7. **Innovative Products:** Returning to his role as a risk-taker, Steve remarked, "We know what is wrong with this company? The current products are holding it back, and there is a lack of excitement in them. We must allocate our resources towards new, futuristic, innovative products.

    In 1998, the iMac was introduced as a $1,299 all-in-one computer. It featured colorful translucent cases with a distinctive eggshell design. Nearly 800,000 units were sold within five months of its launch. Later, 1,350,000 iMacs were sold in just one quarter.

    After a few months, Apple launched the iPod and the iTunes app in 2001. The combination of the iPod and iTunes created a sensation in the music industry. In 2005, a video iPod was released, significantly boosting sales to over 30 million units. Apple generated $10 billion in revenue through the iPod and iTunes alone.

    In 2007, Apple launched the iPhone, which immediately revolutionized the telecom industry. Within a year of its launch, Apple became the world's third-largest supplier of mobile handsets.

    In 2008, Apple released the iPhone and iPod Touch App Store. The App Store generated $1 million daily and sold 60 million apps. Steve Jobs mentioned that our App Store alone is a billion-dollar invention.

    In 2010, Apple launched the iPad, which utilized the iPhone's touch technology and applications. Five hundred thousand iPads were sold in the first week after their launch.

Today, Apple's market capitalization exceeds $700 billion. In 2015, its first-quarter revenue from the iPhone alone reached $51.2 billion, surpassing Yahoo's entire market cap of $45 billion, three times Google's total quarterly revenue, and double Microsoft's total quarterly revenue. Apple possesses $178 billion in cash, more than enough to acquire IBM or to purchase Ford, GM, and Tesla collectively. The company holds twice as much operational cash as the U.S. Treasury. Apple's net income in the last quarter of 2016 was $18 billion.

Strategic Leadership: Howard Schultz at Starbucks

During the subprime crisis in 2008, Starbucks, a leading global coffee shop chain, encountered a significant financial downturn, with its share price crashing by 50%. Howard Schultz, who had stepped down as CEO in 2000, returned to lead Starbucks' turnaround in 2008. The following are the strategic actions that Schultz implemented at Starbucks to facilitate its turnaround.

- He closed over 7,100 stores across the U.S. for three hours to provide training to staff. The training mainly focused on quality coffee and an exceptional customer experience. He placed a sign on the door that read, "We are taking time to perfect our espresso." He trained employees to boil fresh milk only once before preparing coffee to retain the milk's natural sweetness. Training was provided on the optimal grinding of fresh coffee beans just before preparing the coffee. All the trainees were asked to strictly follow the procedures to ensure the same quality every time at every store worldwide. All the employees were encouraged to call customers by their first name, as it adds a personal touch and helps them feel like they are in a familiar place, enhancing their coffee experience.
- Howard permanently shut down 600+ underperforming stores to reduce inefficiencies and maintain the Starbucks brand image.
- To position Starbucks as a tech-savvy retailer, Mr. Howard introduced a mobile ordering and payment system.
- He expanded Starbucks' product line to include healthy food options and premium tea by acquiring Teavana.

Mr. Howard, in his strategic leadership role, recognized that Starbucks needed to do more than serve coffee. He aimed to transform the brand into the best store that delivers an exceptional customer experience, achieved through extraordinary coffee, a welcoming store ambiance, personalized service from employees, and a diverse food menu. Under Howard's excellent leadership strategies, Starbucks's stock quadrupled between 2008 and 2016. The company became the largest coffee shop chain, with 35000 stores worldwide.

ASSESSMENTS

1. What are the differences between managerial and leadership approaches in an organization?
2. Explain the differences between transactional and transformational leadership perspectives.
3. What are the four powers of a transformational leader, and how will you enhance these powers?
4. Critically evaluate autocratic, participative, and free-rein leadership styles.
5. Describe the fundamental steps involved in resolving conflicts within an organization.
6. Please describe various techniques for conducting root cause analysis.
7. Elucidate the various roles of a strategic leader.

CHAPTER 2

Theories of Leadership

Since the start of the Industrial Revolution, many scholars in psychology, sociology, economics, commerce, and business management have been researching the area of leadership to develop leadership models. These models aim to explain how leaders influence individuals, groups, and organizations to achieve their goals. Once these leadership models were tested in real-world situations, they evolved into established leadership theories. In the early stages, leadership theories centered on the traits of leaders and their interactions with subordinates. Subsequent theories concentrated on the actions leaders take to influence individuals and organizations.

This chapter will discuss nine of the most popular and contemporary leadership theories to provide us with the toolkit needed to develop a leadership style best suited to our characteristics, the task at hand, and our situation. The nine leadership theories are as follows:

- Action-Centered Leadership
- Dunham & Pierce's Leadership Process Model
- Fiedler's Contingency Model
- French & Raven's Five Forms of Power
- Hersey-Blanchard Situational Leadership Theory
- Tannenbaum-Schmidt Leadership Continuum
- Path-Goal Theory of Leadership
- Leader-Member Exchange Theory (LMX)
- Zenger & Folkman's 10 Fatal Leadership Flaws

A deeper understanding of leadership theories is essential for demonstrating effective organizational leadership. Today, organizations have a diverse workforce, with individuals possessing different goals and aspirations. It is not feasible to lead everyone using a single leadership model; instead, it is vital to apply various theoretical approaches based on the specific demands of the situation and the differing needs of team members.

2.1 Action-centered Leadership (ACL)

John Adair developed the Action-Centered Leadership Model in 1973. It consists of three elements: Task, Team, and Individual. Leaders must find a balance between tasks, teams, and individuals. However, maintaining this balance can be challenging. The three elements—task, team, and individual—are interdependent and rely on each other for success. This model applies to all levels of the organization, from team leaders to top executives.

1. **Task Accomplishment:** As shown in Figure 2.1, Leaders must define organizational goals, create strategic action plans, develop monitoring processes, and set deadlines for each task. Without tasks, there would be no reason to build a team. Tasks are the guiding force behind the leadership we offer to our followers.

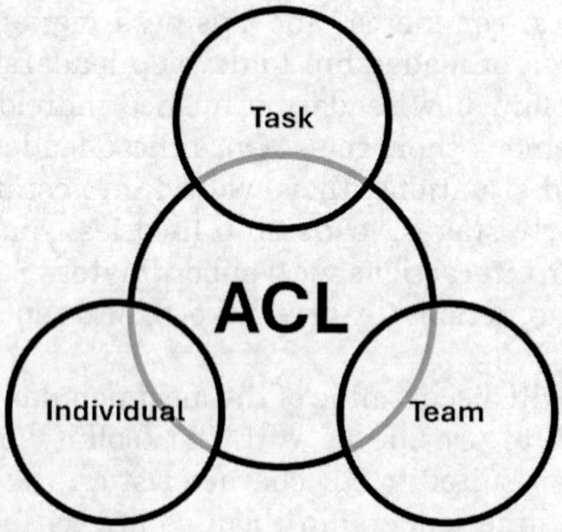

FIGURE 2.1 Action-centered Leadership Model.

2. **Team Building:** Building a competent team is vital for successfully achieving tasks. Leaders foster trust and collaboration among team members and resolve any conflicts that exist between team members. They promote effective communication among team members, encourage participation from everyone, and celebrate success together.
3. **Empowering Individuals:** Many managers commit the common leadership mistake of ignoring team members. Good Leaders understand that individuals have varying degrees of desires, fears, well-being, and motivation that must be addressed for effective team performance. As leaders, we must accept individuals as they are, not as we wish them to be. Recognizing and rewarding their good performance is essential in front of the entire organization. Placing the right people in the right jobs, addressing their needs, and motivating them is key to bringing out the best in each individual.

2.2 Dunham and Pierce's Leadership Process Model

Dunham and Pierce's Leadership Process Model suggests that leadership is not solely about individual traits but a dynamic process influenced by various factors. As shown in Figure 2.2, the model emphasizes four crucial elements essential to the leadership process: the leader, the followers, the context, and the outcomes.

1. **The Leader:** Leaders should possess the traits, skills, and behaviors to lead people effectively. These include emotional intelligence, self-awareness, strong communication skills, and the ability to make sound decisions. Leaders are responsible for generating excellent performance through their followers, who report to them.
2. **The Followers:** A leader without followers is merely walking alone on the street. It is the followers who determine whether leadership is good or bad. We can consider ourselves good leaders only if our followers are willing to follow us again in the future. The trust of followers in a leader, along with their competence and willingness to work, plays a crucial role in achieving the desired outcomes.

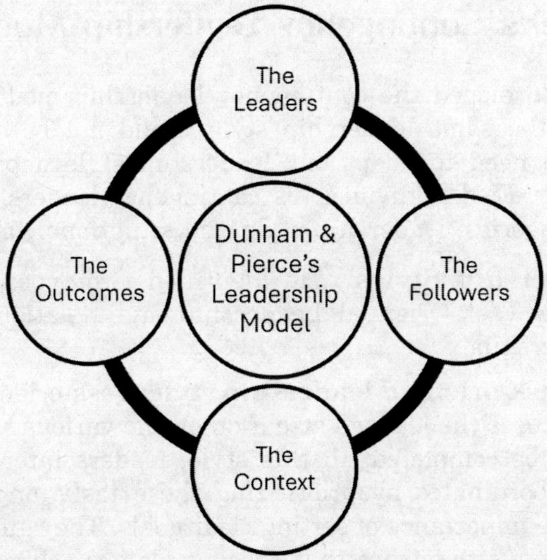

FIGURE 2.2 Dunham & Pierce's Leadership Process Model.

3. **The Context:** Leadership is influenced by the circumstances in which it occurs. Leaders adopt styles depending on organizational culture, task complexity, workload pressure, infrastructural support, inter-departmental coordination, employee relationships, and followers' characteristics and competencies.

4. **The Outcomes:** Leadership effectiveness will only be assessed based on goal achievement, organizational development, team development, and followers' growth and satisfaction.

Fundamental Principles for Implementing this Theory

Examining the four elements of Dunham & Pierce's Leadership Model, leaders must focus on three essential principles: Interaction, Adaptability, and Alignment.

1. **Interaction:** Leaders interact with their followers in the leadership process. They must develop a trusting relationship with their followers and cultivate their potential and willingness to work for the organization.
2. **Adaptability:** As mentioned earlier, leadership does not occur in a vacuum. It takes place in an environment where various factors create a specific situation. Leaders must choose the appropriate leadership style based on the particular situation.
3. **Alignment:** It is crucial to align followers with the organization's goals and action plans to achieve excellent performance outcomes.

2.3 Fiedler's Contingency Leadership Model

Fred Fiedler developed the contingency leadership model in 1960. He believed that the same leadership style would not be effective in all situations. We need to adopt our leadership style depending on the specific context. Fiedler divided his contingency leadership model into two major categories: leadership style and situational favorability.

1. **Leadership Styles:** He identified two types of leadership styles: Task-Oriented Leadership and Relationship-Oriented Leadership.
   - **Task-oriented leadership style:** Task-oriented leadership focuses the leader's attention on the various tasks that need to be completed. In this style, leaders interact with their subordinates by prioritizing these tasks and emphasizing the importance of setting clear goals. They guide employees' actions to ensure that these goals are achieved effectively.

     Fiedler also developed the "Least-Preferred Co-Worker" scale, which assesses a leader's view of their coworkers based on various personality traits, ranked on a scale from 1 to 8. Fiedler assumed that if a leader ranks their coworkers low, it indicates a preference for task-oriented leadership. Conversely, a high ranking suggests a preference for relationship-oriented leadership.

- **Relationship-oriented leadership style:** In a relationship-oriented leadership style, leaders focus on building strong relationships with their subordinates, developing team cohesiveness, and resolving group conflicts.

2. **Situational Favorability:** Fiedler assessed situational favorability based on three factors, which include leader-member relations, task structure, and leader's position power.
   - **Leader-member relations:** What is the level (good or poor) of the relationships between the leader and subordinates regarding trust, respect, and confidence?
   - **Task structure:** The tasks can be structured or unstructured based on their clarity, objectivity, organization, and whether they are closed-ended.
   - **Leader's position power:** How much power (strong or weak) does a leader have regarding the authority to reward, punish, or make decisions?

EXHIBIT 2.1 Fiedler's Contingency Leadership Model

Leadership Style	*Task-Oriented*		*Relationship-Oriented*				*Task-Oriented*	
Situation	*Favorable*		*Moderate*				*Unfavorable*	
Category	1	2	3	4	5	6	7	8
Leader-Member Relation	Good	Good	Good	Good	Good	Good	Good	Good
Task Structure	High	High	Low	Low	High	High	Low	Low
Leader's Position Power	Strong	Weak	Strong	Weak	Strong	Weak	Strong	Weak

3. **Matching Leadership Style with Situational Favorability:** In Exhibit 2.1, Fiedler categorized leadership situations into eight categories based on three factors: leader-member relations (either good or poor), task structure (either high or low), and the leader's position power (either strong or weak). This classification helps match a specific leadership style to the level of situational favorability.

   Further, categories 1 and 2 were considered favorable, categories 3, 4, 5, and 6 were labeled as moderately favorable, and categories 7 and 8 were deemed unfavorable. Fiedler suggests that a task-oriented leadership style leads to high performance in both highly favorable and highly unfavorable situations. In contrast, a relationship-oriented leadership style is most effective in moderately favorable conditions.

Fiedler's contingency leadership theory has been criticized for its rigidity in associating specific leadership styles with situations.

However, it still provides a foundational understanding of the relationship between leadership styles and various situations.

2.4 French and Raven's Five Forms of Power

John French and Bertram Raven researched the five forms of power in 1959 to determine what makes someone powerful in an organizational or social setting. As illustrated in Figure 2.3, they identified five powers: legitimate power, Reward Power, Coercive Power, Expert Power, and Referent Power.

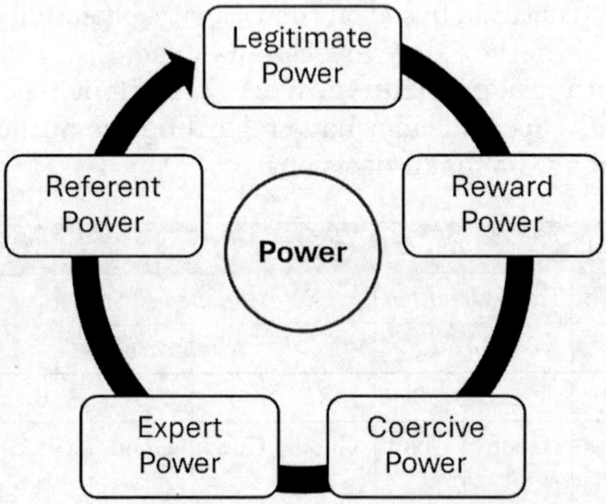

FIGURE 2.3 Five Forms of Power.

1. **Legitimate Power:** Leaders derive legitimate power from their positions within the organization or their roles in social contexts. This authority is formally granted to specific positions or roles. Legitimate power is linked to our position; once we lose that position, our power disappears. For instance, as the CEOs of business organizations, we have the authority to direct all employees to follow specific rules and policies. However, resigning from the CEO position means we can no longer exert the same power.
2. **Reward Power:** Organizational leaders generate power by associating appropriate rewards with employee performance. These rewards can be either tangible or intangible. Tangible rewards include bonuses, salary increases, financial incentives, and promotions. Intangible rewards consist of recognition, praise, and certificates of excellence, among other things.
3. **Coercive Power:** The source of coercive power is the opposite of reward power, where leaders associate poor performance or non-compliance with punishments such as explanation calls,

transfers, fines, salary cuts, demotion, or, in extreme cases, termination.

4. **Expert Power:** Expert power comes from a leader's knowledge, skills, and competencies. People tend to respect leaders who have expertise in their fields. This type of power is long-lasting because it is tied to the individual rather than their position. Consequently, it remains with a person even if they are no longer in a formal leadership role.
5. **Referent Power:** Some leaders generate influence through their personality traits and charisma. People are drawn to them for no logical reason; they simply like them. These charismatic leaders inspire their teams to work towards the organization's vision. They build strong relationships with their followers and maintain a good reputation.

Effective leaders balance all five powers to address intrapersonal and interpersonal conflicts within the organization. They guide individuals toward achieving the organization's vision, mission, and objectives.

Elon Musk's Sources of Power as a Leader

We can easily understand the real-time existence of French and Raven's five forms of power by exploring how many forms of power Mr. Elon Musk embodies as CEO of Tesla and SpaceX.

- Legitimate power is derived from an individual's formal position within an organization. As the CEO of Tesla and SpaceX, Mr. Musk has legitimate power or formal authority over employees, decision-making, and setting the company's direction.
- Expert power arises from a person's knowledge, skills, competencies, and experience. Mr. Musk has extensive knowledge in engineering, physics, and business. This expertise earns him the credibility and trust of people in his decisions.
- Referent power stems from an individual's charisma and ability to influence others through a visionary approach. Mr. Musk has referent power because he has influenced people with his vision of establishing multi-planetary life and his charisma in developing rockets that can travel to space and return safely to the station.
- Mr. Musk generates substantial reward power by regularly offering his employees higher salaries, incentives, bonuses, promotions, and public recognition for their excellent performance.
- Finally, Mr. Musk utilizes his coercive power by regularly firing employees who do not meet high-performance standards in the organization.

2.5 Hersey-Blanchard Situational Leadership Theory

In 1969, Paul Hersey and Ken Blanchard introduced the situational leadership model. This model suggests that leaders should adjust their leadership style based on the maturity levels of their followers, which are determined by their commitment and competence. The main components of situational leadership theory are the leadership style and the maturity levels of the followers, which will be discussed further below:

1. **Leadership Style:** Figure 2.4 illustrates the situational leadership model, which presents four leadership styles labeled S1, S2, S3, and S4, ranging from directive to supportive leadership behavior.
   - **Telling (S1):** Telling is a highly directive and low-supportive behavior. Leaders inform followers about what tasks to complete and how to perform them. Research shows that the Telling leadership style is highly suitable for followers who exhibit low competence and commitment.
   - **Selling (S2):** In the selling leadership style, leaders demonstrate a combination of highly directive and supportive behaviors. The concept of selling stems from leaders needing to persuade some team members on what to do and how to do it.
   - **Participating (S3):** In this leadership style, instead of telling or selling, leaders allow their followers to participate in making decisions about what to do and how to do it.
   - **Delegating (S4):** This style is appropriate when the followers are mature and highly competent to decide what to do and how to do it. Leaders simply delegate the responsibility to their followers.
2. **Followers' Maturity Level:** Hersey and Blanchard identified four maturity levels of followers based on their competence and commitment. They designated these maturity levels with the symbols M1, M2, M3, and M4.

   Figure 2.4 illustrates four maturity levels of followers, determined by varying levels of competence and commitment.
   - **M1:** Low Competence and Low Commitment
   - **M2:** Low Competence and High Commitment
   - **M3:** High Competence and Low Commitment
   - **M4:** High Competence and High Commitment
3. **Application of Hersey and Blanchard Situational Leadership Model:** As illustrated in Figure 2.5, leaders align their leadership styles with the maturity levels of their followers. This alignment is described as follows:

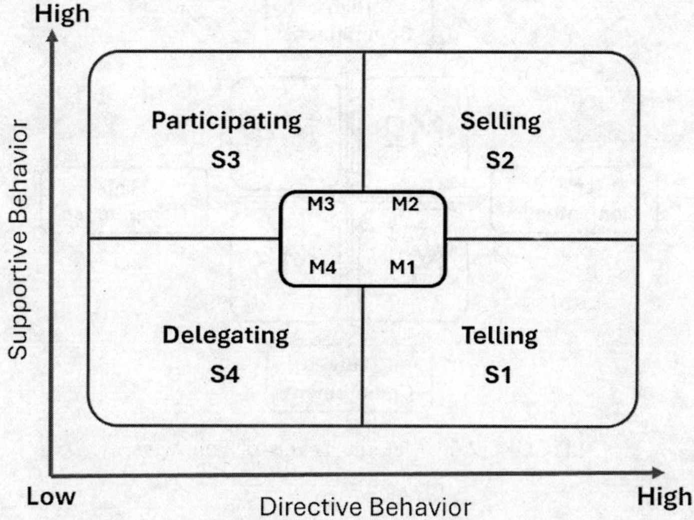

FIGURE 2.4 Hersey-Blanchard Situational Leadership Model.

- **Telling—M1:** At the M1 maturity level, the followers lack competence and commitment to their jobs; therefore, leaders need to micromanage by providing detailed instructions on tasks and actions.
- **Selling—M2:** At the M2 maturity level, followers are committed to their jobs but have low competence. As a result, leaders take the initiative to decide on tasks and action plans themselves. They then sell these plans to their followers, who perform the tasks as instructed.
- **Participating—M3:** At the M3 maturity level, followers are highly skilled at performing tasks but lack commitment to their jobs. Leaders should involve them in decision-making regarding tasks and action plans to win their commitment.
- **Delegating—M4:** At the M4 maturity level, followers are highly skilled and dedicated to their roles. As a result, leaders can delegate overall responsibility to followers to determine what actions to take and how to execute them.

The Hersey and Blanchard situational leadership model allows leaders to adopt different leadership styles based on varying situations. Its straightforward and adaptable approach contributes to its popularity in business organizations and leadership training programs.

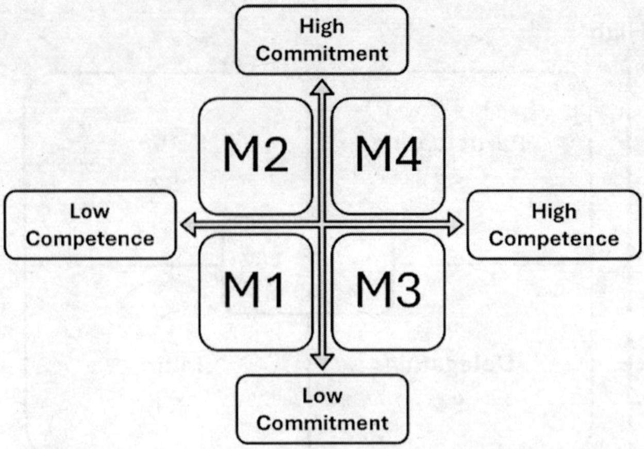

FIGURE 2.5 Maturity Levels of Followers.

2.6 Tannenbaum-Schmidt Leadership Continuum

Robert Tannenbaum and Warren H. Schmidt created the Tannenbaum-Schmidt Leadership Continuum model in 1958 and refined it again in 1973. This model outlines a range of leadership styles based on managers' use of authority and subordinates' areas of freedom. The continuum describes seven levels of leadership behavior, from manager-oriented to team-oriented leadership behavior. The continuum outlines seven leadership behaviors that fall between these two extremes.

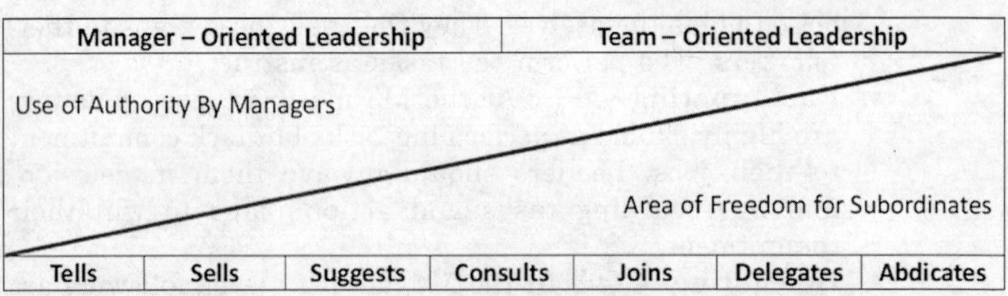

FIGURE 2.6 Tannenbaum-Schmidt Leadership Continuum Model.

Figure 2.6 illustrates the seven leadership behaviors: Tells, Sells, Suggests, Consults, joins, Delegates, and Abdicates. As we move from Telling towards Abdicating, the authority used by managers decreases, creating more freedom for subordinates. The seven leadership behaviors are defined as follows:

1. **Tells:** In this behavior, leaders autocratically make decisions regarding various tasks and action plans and instruct their subordinates to follow them.

2. **Sells:** Under Sell's leadership style, leaders make decisions about various tasks and action plans and persuade their subordinates to complete them.
3. **Suggests:** Under the suggests leadership style, leaders adopt a softer approach and consider suggestions from team members. However, accepting suggestions depends on leaders' trust in their team members' competencies.
4. **Consults:** In a consulting leadership style, leaders are open to incorporating input from their followers when making decisions. They present ideas to their followers and invite feedback to inform their choices. However, the leaders ultimately retain the authority to make the final decision.
5. **Joins:** At this point in the continuum, leaders begin to act as team members rather than as dictators giving orders. This change occurs when a leader is working with a highly competent team.
6. **Delegates:** In a delegating style, leaders grant followers complete authority to make decisions and act within clearly defined boundaries.
7. **Abdicates:** Abdicating leadership behavior refers to leaders relinquishing all control to their teams, trusting them to complete tasks from beginning to end.

2.7 Path-Goal Theory of Leadership

Robert House developed the path-goal theory of Leadership in 1971. This theory suggests that leaders help their subordinates set job-related goals, develop action plans to achieve them, and provide guidance and support to overcome obstacles. Additionally, leaders should reward their subordinates to keep them motivated. In doing so, leaders adopt one of the four leadership styles based on the followers' situation, task complexity, and competencies. As shown in Figure 2.7, the path-goal theory of leadership revolves around two dimensions: the leader's responsibilities and leadership styles.

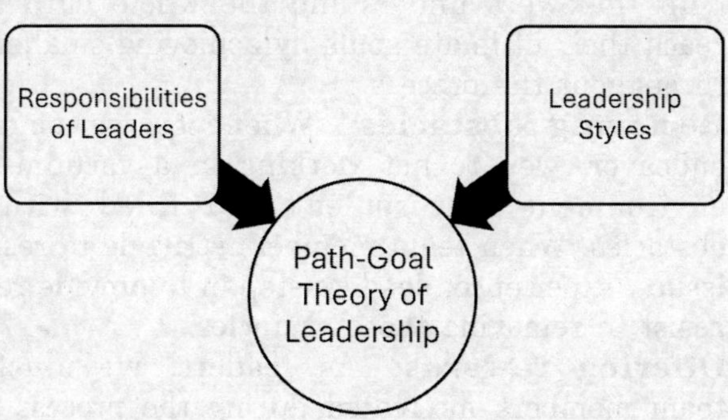

FIGURE 2.7 Path-Goal Theory of Leadership.

According to the path-goal theory, leaders have three primary responsibilities and utilize four distinct leadership styles to fulfill these responsibilities. Figure 2.8 provides a comprehensive presentation of the path-goal theory. The figure consists of two circles: inner and outer circles. The inner circle highlights three key responsibilities of leaders: clearing the path, removing obstacles, and offering rewards. The outer circle outlines four leadership styles: directive, participative, supportive, and achievement-oriented leadership.

FIGURE 2.8 Leader's Responsibilities and Leadership Styles.

1. **Leader's Responsibilities:** The path-goal theory of leadership outlines three key responsibilities that leaders must fulfill.
   - **Clearing the path:** Experienced leaders have a clear vision of the entire path from start to finish, which can be challenging for inexperienced followers to visualize. Leaders assist their followers in figuring out end goals and identifying small milestones along the way. This approach helps followers understand the whole path and how to reach their ultimate goals by achieving smaller milestones throughout the process.
   - **Removing obstacles:** Whenever we engage in any endeavor, we are not working in a vacuum. Today, the environment is turbulent and filled with numerous obstacles. When team members struggle to resolve various issues, experienced leaders step in to provide resources and assist in removing those obstacles.
   - **Offering rewards:** As leaders, we must keep our team members motivated during the process and remain

motivated even after completing the task. Leaders show genuine appreciation for team members' dedication and provide financial rewards upon completing the task. They also offer appreciation letters to high performers.

2. **Leadership Styles:** Leaders may choose any of the four leadership styles recommended in the path-goal theory to fulfill their three responsibilities. The four leadership styles are described in the following texts.

   - **Directive leadership:** In directive leadership, leaders give clear instructions and deadlines to their subordinates, expecting them to complete tasks according to those instructions. Leaders have complete control over adopting this style of leadership. They adopt this style when the task is complex, and the followers are somewhat inexperienced.
   - **Participative leadership:** When subordinates are experienced and competent enough to perform tasks, leaders involve them in decision-making. Participative leadership helps leaders build collaboration with subordinates and gain their commitment. Subordinates feel empowered and remain motivated to achieve success.
   - **Supportive leadership:** When subordinates take on significant responsibility for setting tasks, developing strategies for success, and taking action to accomplish those tasks, leaders tend to become more supportive. They focus on meeting each subordinate's needs, creating a supportive environment, and providing all necessary resources to help achieve the task.
   - **Achievement-oriented leadership:** In this leadership style, leaders prioritize developing their subordinates' skills to help them become high achievers. They establish challenging goals, provide mentorship, boost their confidence, and support them in achieving extraordinary results.

How Ford Motors Utilized the Path-Goal Theory of Leadership?
Around 2015, Ford Motors faced numerous challenges, including market competition, evolving technologies, and a significant need for restructuring. To overcome these challenges, Ford's leaders applied the principles of the Pat-Goal theory. In a span of five years, they redirected their focus towards the design and production of electric vehicles (EVs). Effective communication from leaders at all levels helped clarify goals and action plans for all employees. As a result, every employee clearly understood the path forward and the various steps involved in achieving EV vehicle production.

To eliminate all barriers, Ford announced an $11.4 billion investment in electric vehicle manufacturing and communicated clear roles and performance expectations to all teams involved. Ford's leadership emphasized creating a supportive work environment. They showed empathy, fostered a sense of security among employees, and successfully addressed all their concerns.

Ford promoted teamwork and encouraged input from all team members involved in product development. For example, when creating new electric vehicle models, leaders have included input from engineers, designers, and assembly-line workers.

Ford set ambitious goals to become a leader in the EV market and began rewarding employees for their innovative ideas and exceptional performance.

In late 2020, Ford made a significant entry into the EV market by launching its first all-electric SUV, the Mustang Mach-E. Later, in spring 2022, Ford introduced an all-electric F-150 pickup truck, which became its best-selling product. Still, Ford Motors is investing significantly in electric vehicles and aims to reach carbon neutrality by 2050.

2.8 Leader-Member Exchange Theory (LMX)

Leader-Member Exchange (LMX) theory, also known as the Vertical Dyad Linkage theory, was developed by George Graen and colleagues. This theory focuses on the relationship between leaders and their followers. The following are the key components of LMX theory:

1. **Dyadic Relationship:** The LMX theory focuses on the dyadic relationship, which refers to a one-on-one connection between a leader and a follower. The term "dyad" indicates an interdependent pair, meaning that the actions and emotions of one person influence the other. In the workplace, this dyadic relationship can vary from highly intimate to more formal.
2. **In-Group and Out-Group:** Followers are categorized into the in-group and the out-group based on intimacy in the leader-follower relationship. In-group members enjoy high-quality exchanges with their leader, leading to increased responsibilities, support, and growth opportunities. They have greater access to resources and are often invited to participate in organizational decision-making. In contrast, out-group members experience low-quality exchanges with the leader. Their relationship is more formal and transactional, resulting in limited access to resources, inadequate support, and fewer growth opportunities.
3. **Impact on Performance:** High-quality leader-member exchange (LMX) relationships lead to improved performance, increased job satisfaction, more significant organizational commitment, and lower turnover rates. Conversely, low-

quality LMX relationships result in poor performance, job dissatisfaction, and higher turnover rates.

4. **Implications for Leaders:** The LMX theory proposes that maintaining high-quality exchanges with followers can improve team performance, job satisfaction, and overall organizational success. Leaders should strive to build high-quality relationships with as many followers as possible while minimizing the number of out-group members. To achieve this, leaders must be fair and supportive to all followers, offering them equal opportunities for growth and development. Additionally, leaders should recognize the individual needs of each follower and provide appropriate mentoring support.

2.9 Zenger and Folkman's 10 Fatal Leadership Flaws

Zenger and Folkman conducted extensive research on leadership effectiveness using 360-degree assessments of thousands of leaders. They identified ten critical leadership flaws that contribute to failures in leadership. The ten fatal leadership flaws are discussed below:

1. **Lack of Energy and Enthusiasm:** A leader's primary responsibility is to inspire and motivate people to work diligently. If a team member lacks energy and enthusiasm, a leader can uplift and energize them. However, suppose leaders themselves are low on energy. In that case, it negatively affects the entire work environment and diminishes the team's motivation. Employees become disengaged, stop believing in their leaders' vision, and stop following their instructions. Lack of energy and enthusiasm negatively impacts a leader's ability to guide their team in a crisis and overcome various challenges. Therefore, leaders must maintain their energy and enthusiasm to maintain their team morale.
2. **Accept Own Mediocre Performance:** When leaders begin to accept their mediocre performance, it has significant negative consequences for themselves, their teams, and the entire organization. Leaders who settle for mediocrity lose the respect and trust of their people, which ultimately affects their credibility. Employees begin to see average performance as the standard for excellence and rate their performance as excellent. As a result, a culture of complacency is created due to the lack of challenges that promote real excellence. Average employees are often appreciated, leading to high-performing team members leaving the organization. In today's highly competitive environment, the survival of low-performing organizations becomes nearly impossible.

3. **Lack of Clear Vision and Direction:** According to Mr. Jack Welch, one of the most successful CEOs of the modern business era, incredible leaders create a vision, passionately own it, articulate it to others, and relentlessly drive it forward. A compelling vision is an excellent tool to align people with organizational activities. Without it, leaders and employees become directionless and disengaged. In the absence of clear direction, the organizational resources, such as time, money, and talents, are wasted. Their utilization becomes haphazard, causing the organization to move blindly in an uncertain direction.
4. **Have Poor Judgment:** In today's information-driven world, all business organizations strive for accurate analysis to make effective decisions regarding market size, demand, employee hiring, costing, pricing, and marketing communication. Poor judgment regarding people and businesses can lead to poor choices by leaders, ultimately affecting the organization's productivity, profitability, and growth. The essence of leadership is for leaders to be available to make difficult choices that enhance the organization's productivity, profitability, and development.
5. **Do Not Collaborate:** Effective leaders recognize that collaboration provides valuable insights from experts across various fields, enhancing the organization's strength and sustainability. Due to their position, ineffective leaders often adopt a know-it-all attitude, making them reluctant to collaborate with knowledgeable individuals. This absence of collaboration deprives the organization of valuable insights from experts.
6. **Do Not Walk the Talk:** As leaders, we must ensure that our actions are aligned with what we say, believe, and promise. In other words, it emphasizes that we must practice what we preach. When leaders fail to follow their standards, cynicism increases. Employees develop a "why bother?" attitude, eroding organizational culture.

   Effective leaders are recognized as integrated human beings. How can someone be considered an integrated human being if they do not align their practices with what they preach to others? Failing to walk the talk results in customers, partners, and other stakeholders losing confidence in the organization.
7. **Resist New Ideas:** Poor leaders are often stubborn and closed-minded to new ideas. In contrast, visionary leaders remain receptive to innovative thoughts. New ideas can drive innovation, enhance organizational growth, and achieve remarkable outcomes.
8. **Do Not Learn from Mistakes:** Many great leaders have said that our mistakes and failures are great teachers, and we

learn a lot from them. In other words, failures are stepping stones that we walk on to achieve ultimate success. However, instead of learning from mistakes and taking corrective measures for the next time, poor leaders always try to find excuses and look for scapegoats to blame them. Those who refuse to acknowledge their mistakes will likely repeat them, perpetuating a cycle of failure. This continuous cycle of failure ensures that organizational resources are wasted, leading to stagnation or a decline in the organization's progress.

9. **Lack of Interpersonal Skills:** At its core, leadership revolves around interpersonal skills. A leader can communicate effectively, interact, and build productive relationships with subordinates. Interpersonal skills are essential for leaders to resolve conflicts, mentor and nurture subordinates, motivate them, and create a positive work environment. Lack of interpersonal skills in leaders leads to escalation of conflicts, reduced trust levels between leaders and subordinates, decreased organizational productivity, and higher employee turnover.
10. **Fail to Develop Others:** As a leader, if we believe we are indispensable to the organization, then we are not a good leader. Good leaders always look for ways to develop and transform their subordinates into great leaders. Teaching, mentoring, and counseling are essential functions of leaders, through which they nurture their subordinates and transform them into extraordinary individuals. Poor leaders fear losing their position, which makes them hesitant to develop their subordinates, resulting in organizations that remain average and stagnant.

Zenger and Folkman's *10 Fatal Leadership Flaws* is a must-read for anyone in a leadership position. If we identify any of these flaws in our performance, we should take the necessary steps to improve in those areas and work towards becoming great leaders.

ASSESSMENTS

1. Describe the action-centered leadership model using suitable examples.
2. Please explain Dunham and Pierce's leadership model.
3. Explain Fiedler's contingency leadership model using appropriate examples.
4. Explain the five forms of power identified by French and Raven within the organization. How will you optimize these powers?
5. With suitable examples, explain the path-goal theory of leadership.
6. Describe the leader-member exchange (LMX) theory of leadership.
7. Elucidate Zenger and Folkman's 10 fatal leadership flaws.

CHAPTER 3

Leader as an Integrated Human Being

Today, the entire world seeks leaders who are integrated individuals. Integrated leaders exhibit brilliant personality traits and skills. They are proactive, visionary, and emotionally intelligent, demonstrating compassion for their subordinates. They have outstanding emotional intelligence and interpersonal skills that cultivate productive relationships with others, leading to remarkable organizational performance. To become an exceptional leader, one must go beyond simply adopting various leadership approaches and fulfilling their functions. We must integrate distinctive attributes into our personality and develop specific skills to elevate ourselves from average leaders to great leaders.

3.1 Key Attributes of a Leader

Figure 3.1 illustrates some key attributes that define great leaders.

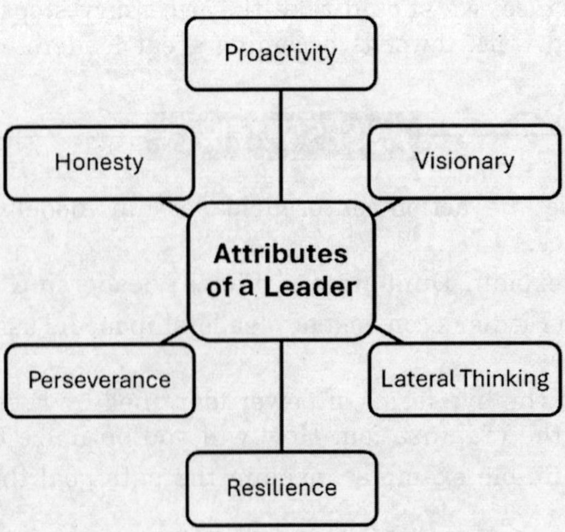

FIGURE 3.1 Attributes of a Leader.

3.1.1 Proactivity

Proactivity means taking charge of your life and creating a pathway to success. Effective leaders are proactive. Instead of waiting for changes to occur and merely reacting to them, proactive leaders anticipate future changes and challenges and take proactive steps to align the organization accordingly. They shape ideas rather than simply responding to them. They do not wait for external triggers but take the initiative to make things happen. They concentrate on their role within the organization rather than on protecting their position. They view themselves as accountable for what occurs within the organization and address potential issues before they escalate into problems. They actively envision a future for the organization and set goals out of passion rather than necessity. Proactive leaders do not wait for opportunities; instead, they focus on creating them. They implement changes to the system for improvement. They possess a remarkable ability to manage their circumstances as they consistently develop new approaches.

1. *Proactive Model based on Stimulus Response Theory*

Viktor Frankl (1984) developed a proactive model based on the stimulus-response theory. As shown in Figure 3.2, Frankl believed that reactive individuals respond spontaneously to external stimuli, allowing these stimuli to dictate their actions. They usually react favorably when presented with positive stimuli, whereas negative stimuli provoke adverse responses. Their reactions are primarily shaped by their surroundings.

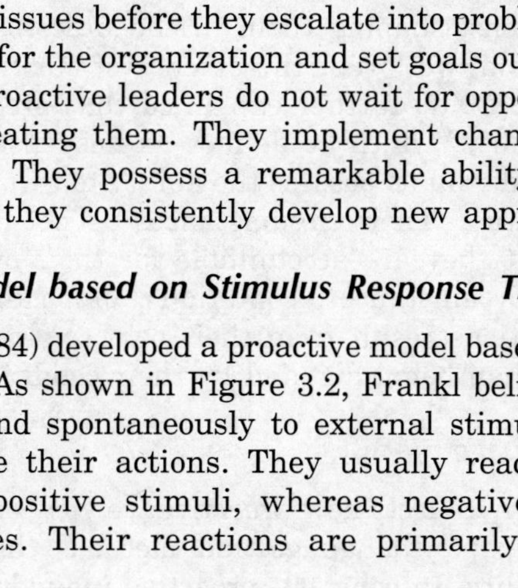

FIGURE 3.2 Reactive Model.

However, as illustrated in Figure 3.3, Viktor Frankl stated, "Between the stimulus and response lies a space. In that space resides our freedom and the power to choose our response. Proactive individuals utilize this space to select their responses. The stimulus does not dictate their responses; they arise from their conscience. Proactive individuals can choose responses based on their self-awareness, imagination, conscience, and independent will. No one can take away our power to choose our response in any situation."

In other words, no one can control our emotions and thoughts unless we permit them to. Our growth and happiness depend on our responses. According to Frankl's teachings, we are not victims of our circumstances; instead, we are victims of our reactions to those circumstances. We hold the power to choose our attitudes and responses

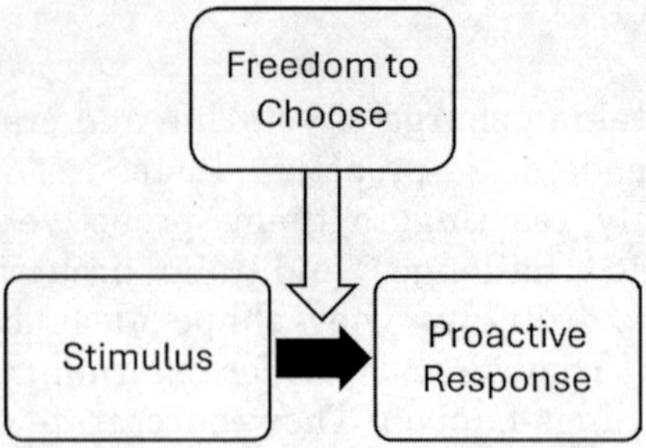

FIGURE 3.3 Proactive Response Model.

toward our situations, shaping them in the process. If we neglect to exercise this freedom, we forfeit the essence of our lives.

Steven Covey (1997) further explained that proactive individuals possess 'Responsibility,' which he defines as Response + Ability, which means proactive individuals possess the ability to respond appropriately in any given situation. Their circumstances do not control them, and they recognize that they are accountable for their own lives; they do not blame their circumstances, conditions, or conditioning for their behavior. Their actions result from their own conscious choices based on values rather than being dictated by their conditions.

2. *Proactive Language*

Our language clearly reflects how proactive we view ourselves. Reactive individuals often employ language and methods that diminish their sense of responsibility. In contrast, proactive individuals use language and strategies that embrace responsibility. Exhibit 3.1 illustrates the different languages and methods reactive and proactive individuals use.

EXHIBIT 3.1 Reactive and Proactive Language and Approach

Reactive Language	*Proactive Language*
• There is nothing I can do.	• Let us examine our alternatives.
• That is just the way I am.	• I can choose a different approach.
• He makes me so mad.	• I have control over my feelings.
• He will not allow that.	• I can develop a compelling presentation.
• I have to do that.	• I will choose an appropriate response.
• I cannot; that is me.	• Let us look at what we can do.
• I have to do it.	• I prefer to do it.
• If only I had a more generous boss.	• I can be more flexible and cooperative.
• If I had a better position in the organization.	• I can be more innovative and sincere.

(*Contd.*)

Reactive Approach	*Proactive Approach*
• I disagree with your point.	• Your point seems interesting.
• You have given a foolish idea.	• Interesting idea.
• This cannot be done.	• Let us find out what can be done.
• Reactive individuals use 'will not,' which is the word of withdrawal.	• Proactive individuals use the word 'did,' which is the word for accomplishment.
• They use the word 'cannot,' which is a word of defeat.	• They use the word 'can,' a word of authority.

Elon Musk's Proactive Leadership Approach

An excellent example of a proactive approach is Elon Musk, the CEO of Tesla and SpaceX. Musk set ambitious, seemingly impossible goals for SpaceX, which included developing reusable rockets and making humanity a multi-planetary species by establishing a colony of humans on Mars. These goals represent his proactive response to Earth's existential risks in the future. Musk proactively invested in developing SpaceX's engines and reusable rockets (Falcon 9). He has successfully achieved the goal of creating a reusable rocket, which revolutionized space travel by significantly cutting costs. Musk's proactive leadership is characterized by his ability to see the invisible and achieve what seems impossible. The reusable rockets and global satellite internet (Starlink) exemplify his exceptional abilities.

3.1.2 Visionary

Great leaders possess a remarkable ability to see the invisible. They can clearly visualize the future scenario of the organization and create strategies to turn that vision into reality. According to Costa and McCrae's Five-Factor Model (FFM) of Personality Traits, "Openness to Experience" is a trait that makes a person both visionary and open to new ideas and methods. Visionary individuals think ahead, paint a compelling picture of the future, and inspire others by aligning them emotionally with their painted future picture. They challenge the status quo through their vision, creating an environment where creativity can thrive. Visionary leaders take their people to a place they have never been before. According to one of the most successful CEOs of the modern business era, Mr. Jack Welch, incredible leaders create the vision, passionately own and articulate that vision to others, and relentlessly drive the vision.

Reed Hastings' (Netflix) Visionary Approach

Wilmot Reed Hastings Jr. is a co-founder and the executive chairman of Netflix, Inc. He envisioned a future in which entertainment would be accessible online on demand, breaking away from the limitations of traditional television. He began transforming a DVD rental store into an online entertainment platform to achieve this vision. Hastings' vision transformed the entertainment industry and established global standards for streaming services. Netflix expanded to over 190 countries and became a leader in global entertainment.

3.1.3 Lateral Thinking

Leaders and their teams are actively involved in envisioning their organizations' future and developing strategies to achieve it. This complex process demands exceptional creativity and innovation, which requires leaders to have lateral thinking skills.

Dr. Edward De Bono introduced the concept of lateral thinking to the world through his well-known book, *Lateral Thinking*. In this book, he explains the distinction between vertical and lateral thinking and how lateral thinking can be applied to foster invention and innovation.

According to him, our minds are habitually vertical thinkers, functioning as continuous, self-maximizing systems for pattern recognition. In vertical thinking, we tend to immediately judge each alternative and polarize the information, ensuring that each step is correct and properly linked to the previous one. Our subconscious quickly rejects any idea that does not align with previously stored information. Vertical thinking compels us to always move forward in search of the single most likely solution.

In contrast, lateral thinking allows us to break free from established patterns. We can move backward, forward, or even flip our perspective. We can rearrange information differently and postpone early judgments and polarization. It focuses on generating multiple approaches by processing the same information in various ways while suspending judgment of right or wrong. Lateral thinking can be implemented through specific techniques:

(a) **Generation of choices:** Lateral thinking focuses on generating multiple options or alternative solutions by rearranging and restructuring the same information in different ways. Rather than searching for a single best perspective on a problem, we should approach it from various angles and articulate it in multiple ways.

For example, regarding the problem of the water crisis, we can frame several statements such as:

- We are experiencing a water crisis due to poor rainfall
- A low underground water table exacerbates the crisis
- Over-extraction of underground water contributes to the issue
- The lack of water storage facilities plays a significant role, and
- The absence of rainwater harvesting systems further intensifies the problem.

One approach to generating alternatives is to appreciate the various perspectives on the same situation, person, or object. For instance, the higher failure rate in board exams can be interpreted in different ways:

- A higher failure rate could be viewed as a positive development because it raises the quality standards in the education system across the country.
- It may be beneficial because students will become more serious about their studies.
- Conversely, a higher failure rate could be harmful because it might decrease students' motivation.
- Moreover, the higher failure rate in the board exams could be seen as harmful, as the country might encounter a workforce crisis.

By exploring these diverse viewpoints, we can better understand the issue at hand.

(b) **Challenge and Question Everything:** A consensus on any philosophy, assumption, rule, norm, policy, or phenomenon does not guarantee that they are correct. For example, most scientists historically believed that Earth's gravitational force was a pull generated from its core until Einstein challenged this idea. He demonstrated that gravitational force is, in fact, a push from the space matrix toward the Earth. Similarly, scientists once believed that space and time were two separate entities until Einstein's theory of special relativity revealed that they are, in fact, one. To foster innovation, we must cultivate a habit of questioning everything.

(c) **No Block is the Biggest Block:** Sometimes, our creativity and desire for change are blocked because the road we are on is smooth and without obstacles. There are no hindrances in our way. The best time for change is not during a crisis; instead, we should seek change when everything is calm. When everything is smooth, our minds try to find shortcuts to rearrange the pattern.

For instance, when asked to arrange three parallelograms, many of us will arrange them in a sequential layout, as illustrated in Figure 3.4. This is because there is typically no incentive to search for a better solution when an adequate one is readily available.

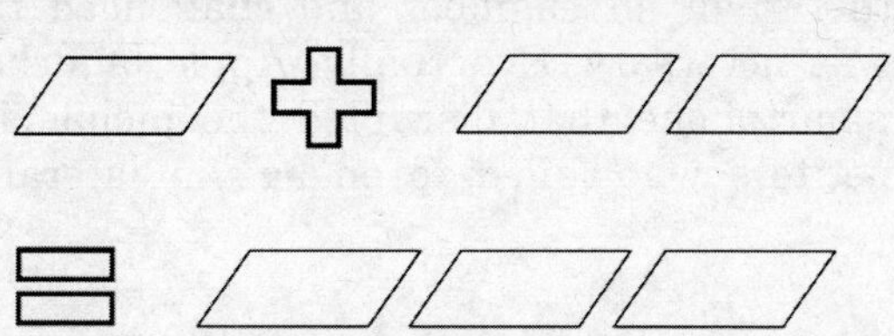

FIGURE 3.4 Linking Three Parallelograms.

In contrast, an innovator would explore alternatives and arrange the three pieces into a box, as shown in Figure 3.5.

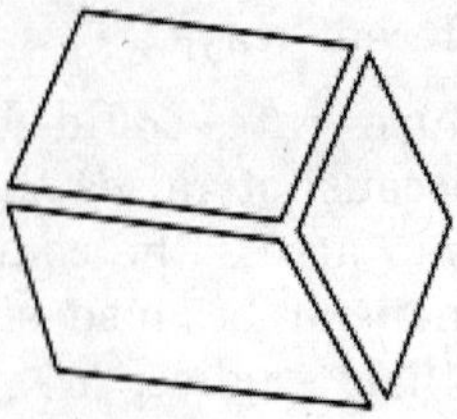

FIGURE 3.5 Alternative Way of Linking Three Parallelograms.

We have developed methods to address issues, but have not established methods for managing what is already sufficient. This oversight can result in complacency, carelessness, stubbornness, overconfidence, and lethargy.

Large companies, such as Nokia, General Motors, and Eastman Kodak, lost their market positions because they failed to recognize the need for change. They became complacent and hesitated to modify their product lines due to their confidence in their substantial customer base.

When gasoline was invented, there was little research or innovation focused on batteries, as gasoline was easy to use and readily available in ample quantities. However, with the increasing concern about global warming, there is a growing interest in developing batteries that can store large amounts of energy.

In addition to describing three techniques used in lateral thinking, two other techniques are also employed in the process. These techniques include creating a fishbone diagram and fractionation, which were already discussed in Chapter 1.

Steve Jobs's Lateral Thinking and iPhone Touchscreen

In the early 2000s, mobile phones were dominated by physical keypads, and manufacturers sought to enhance them in terms of size, functionality, keypad cover, and more. The leading players in the mobile handset industry were Nokia and BlackBerry. Apple was researching touchscreen technology for the iPad, a smaller version of laptops. Steve Jobs wondered why this technology couldn't be applied to mobile handsets. At the time, many people believed that a physical keypad was essential for mobile phones. However, Steve thought like a consumer rather than an engineer and challenged the assumption that a keypad was necessary. Eventually, Apple launched the iPhone, a touchscreen smartphone that disrupted the mobile industry. They surpassed competitors who failed to engage in lateral thinking and adapt quickly.

3.1.4 Resilience

We are not operating in isolation, nor is our business on a simple, straightforward path. Today's environment is turbulent and filled with challenges. As leaders, we are responsible for guiding our organizations through these difficulties to achieve their goals. Along the way, we will face many ups and downs and obstacles that cannot be overcome with a rigid approach. Instead, we must be flexible and adaptable, bending in the direction of the prevailing challenges while seeking the best way to move forward. Resilience is adopting this flexible mindset, allowing for recovery and strength in the face of adversity. Great leaders are highly resilient; they recognize that a rigid approach can lead to failure when confronted with challenging circumstances.

Ford's Resilient Approach to Avoid Bankruptcy during the 2008 Recession

During the 2008 subprime financial crisis, U.S. automakers such as General Motors and Chrysler declared bankruptcy. However, Ford Motors survived without government bailout funds due to its resilient approach. Ford secured $23 billion in loans to ensure liquidity before the crisis hit. The company redesigned its vehicles to enhance fuel efficiency and integrate better technology. They became leaner by divesting non-core brands like Jaguar and Land Rover and streamlining operations. They adopted the "One Ford" strategy to unify their global operations. This approach kept them afloat during the crisis period, and soon after, they posted record profits and continued to be one of the leading global automakers.

3.1.5 Perseverance

Perseverance is the ability to keep going despite challenges, obstacles, and setbacks. It is a never-quit attitude that provides the strength to push through difficulties and move forward. It equips leaders with the mental toughness, adaptability, and determination to survive in a chaotic environment. Great leaders are sufficiently perseverant to remain committed to their goals, even when facing challenges. While leading organizations, leaders often encounter deadlock in situations where quitting seems easy; however, great leaders continue to navigate the turbulent path and ultimately achieve the desired results. By staying persistent, they maintain their momentum and enthusiasm over time. Leaders who demonstrate perseverance can build trust and credibility among their team members, stakeholders, and peers. Perseverant leaders show determination that inspires their team members to stay committed and work harder, helping them maintain momentum and enthusiasm over time. They earn respect and recognition both within their organization and throughout the industry.

3.1.6 Honesty

Honesty is being truthful. It reflects a person's integrity and reliability. Honest leaders establish the tone for ethical behavior within an organization. They encourage open communication and transparency, fostering a culture where information is shared freely. This approach reduces both intrapersonal and interpersonal conflicts while enhancing creativity and innovation. Honest leaders take responsibility for their organizations and hold themselves accountable for their decisions and actions. By promoting a culture of accountability, they instill a sense of ownership in their subordinates. Being truthful eliminates the need to remember what we have said on various occasions, significantly reduces our stress and conflicts, and increases our credibility and reliability with others. Honest communication from leaders also minimizes ambiguity and stress among team members.

3.2 Interpersonal Skills of a Leader

Good interpersonal skills are essential for leaders to align people with their vision, inspire them to drive change within the organization, build productive teams, motivate team members to stay engaged in their roles, and foster a high-performance organizational culture. As shown in Figure 3.6, leaders can develop their interpersonal skills by focusing on four key elements: emotional intelligence, communication skills, compassion, and creating synergy.

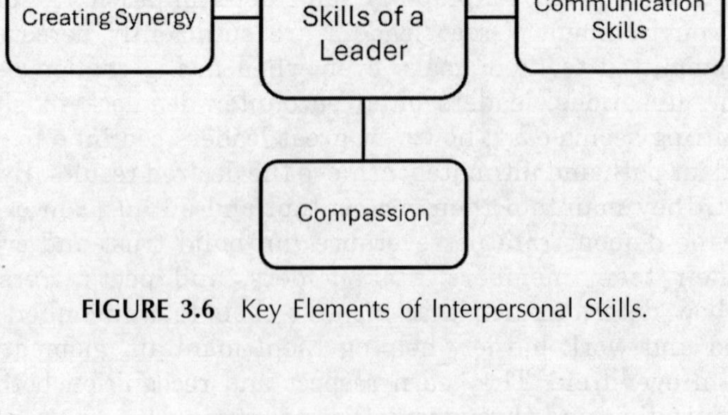

FIGURE 3.6 Key Elements of Interpersonal Skills.

3.2.1 Emotional Intelligence

1. *Understanding Emotions*

An emotion is a powerful feeling, like love, fear, anger, or hatred, that arises from our situations, moods, or relationships. In psychology, emotion is often described as a complex feeling that leads to both physical and psychological changes, affecting our thoughts and behaviors. Emotions are closely linked to our thinking, temperament, personality, mood, and motivation. When we encounter a stimulus, certain neurochemicals are released in our limbic brain in response. The specific combination of these neurochemicals produces particular emotions or feelings.

Reptiles like crocodilians, snakes, and lizards show only very basic emotional expressions, such as fear, aggression, and mating instincts. They are generally not very social creatures due to their lack of more complex emotions. Their survival largely depends on these rudimentary feelings. In contrast, humans possess a highly developed emotional brain capable of producing a variety of chemical reactions, leading to a wide spectrum of emotions that range from extremely negative to extremely positive. We have developed the ability to maintain a specific emotional state for extended periods, whether positive or negative. Emotions can be broadly categorized into two types: positive and negative.

Positive emotions are feelings that we generally find rewarding to experience. In their book, the *Oxford Handbook of Positive Psychology*, Cohn and Fredrickson define positive emotions as "pleasant or desirable situational responses." Moreover, Watson and Clark explain that positive affectivity is an emotional state marked by frequent feelings of cheerfulness, enthusiasm, and energy.

According to Martin Seligman, positive emotions can be categorized into past, present, and future emotions. The past positive emotions could be satisfaction, gratitude, contentment, fulfillment, pride, or serenity. Future emotions include faith, optimism, hope, confidence, etc.

Present emotions can be categorized into momentary pleasures, such as physical pleasures, and more enduring gratifications. Physical pleasures include experiences derived from sex, delightful fragrances, and delicious food. In contrast, higher-order pleasures encompass feelings of bliss, comfort, and ecstasy. We tend to experience a more lasting sense of gratification when we become fully immersed in activities like reading, teaching, singing, or playing musical instruments. This state of deep engagement is often referred to as the "flow experience."

Dr. Rick Hanson, a renowned neuroscientist, states that positive emotions help organize the brain as a whole and yield extensive benefits, including encouraging 'exploratory behavior' that enhances our mood, boosts optimism and resilience, mitigates trauma, strengthens the immune system, and shields the cardiovascular system from stress. Additionally, it fosters our inner strength, encompassing virtues such as openness, confidence, emotional intelligence, and curiosity.

Negative emotions are those we typically do not find pleasurable to experience. According to Pam, negative emotions can be defined as "unpleasant or unhappy feelings that arise in individuals as a response to an event, experience, or person." These emotions can make us feel depressed and bring us down. In our daily lives, we are exposed to stress hormones about 80 percent of the time, which contribute to our negative or survival emotions, such as fear, anger, anxiety, frustration, depression, sadness, resentment, competition, dislike, hatred, bitterness, and rivalry. Cognitive psychologists refer to this negative emotional state as 'negative affectivity.'

Although negative emotions like fear and anger are essential for our survival and protection in adverse situations and from external threats, maintaining a state of continuous stress for an extended period can impact our cognitive abilities and physical health.

According to Dr. Rick, nearly all of us experience survival emotions due to our negative bias. As our ancestors evolved, avoiding threats proved more crucial for survival than obtaining rewards. We learn more rapidly from pain than from pleasure, making it easy to develop learned helplessness. Sensitization to negative experiences occurs quickly because of cortisol, while positive experiences tend to fade from our memories. The limbic or emotional brain influences the functioning of the neocortex (the conscious mind) as well as the cerebellum. Therefore, it is essential to keep our emotional brain balanced by utilizing our emotional intelligence.

2. *Understanding Emotional Intelligence*

The more we connect with our unexpressed emotions, the more easily we can cultivate our emotional intelligence. Our emotional intelligence fosters emotional independence and enables us to influence others' emotions by mastering emotional reciprocation. Most individuals with high emotional intelligence possess a well-developed understanding of themselves and leverage that self-awareness to become individuals of strong character. They are aware of their thoughts, moods, and feelings. They have strong self-control over their emotional impulses and are aware of the effects of noxious emotions. They also have highly developed social skills and can harmonize with people.

Emotional intelligence is the ability to recognize and manage one's own positive or negative emotions, as well as the emotions of others, in significant interpersonal relationships. A person with emotional intelligence can better control their emotional expressions and engage in relationships wisely and compassionately.

According to Daniel Goleman, a person who is emotionally intelligent and has emotional self-control can remain calm and composed in stressful situations. Emotional stability plays a significant role in recognizing our positive thoughts and managing stress. In the presence of negative emotions like fear, anger, sadness, anxiety, and depression, we are unable to tap into our positive inner resources. Great leaders are emotionally intelligent, which distinguishes them from others. They are self-aware, intrinsically motivated, and possess exceptional social skills. Emotionally intelligent leaders can manage their negative emotions, which often arise when they face challenging situations.

3. *Emotional Hijack*

Daniel Goleman coined the term "amygdala hijack" in his book, *Emotional Intelligence*. The amygdala is part of our emotional brain, which regulates the fight-or-flight response to intense, stressful stimuli. It reacts irrationally in highly stressful situations. The prefrontal cortex (PFC) is part of our thinking brain and oversees our rational thought processes. The amygdala is quick, responding within 15 milliseconds, while the prefrontal cortex is slower, taking about 100 milliseconds to react.

The strong signal that comes into our brain from the eyes or ears goes directly to the thalamus, which then redirects the signals to the amygdala and prefrontal cortex (PFC). However, this signal always reaches the amygdala first because it is much closer to the thalamus. When we encounter an extremely intense and negative stimulus, the amygdala quickly responds to this intensity, impairing PFC functioning by depriving it of a significant portion of blood and oxygen. As a result, we become emotionally hijacked, and our neocortex (thinking brain) becomes deactivated due to a lack of sufficient blood and oxygen. In this emotionally hijacked state, our emotional brain starts to dominate and guide our thinking brain.

Matthew Lieberman, a neuroscientist, has discovered an inverse relationship between the amygdala and the prefrontal cortex (PFC). When the amygdala draws more blood and oxygen while there is less activation in the PFC, we can lose 10 to 15 IQ points temporarily, which explains the "What was I thinking?" phenomenon. This is why we struggle to think clearly when we are emotionally charged or unstable. We begin to think irrationally due to our negative emotions. If we assess our daily mental state, we will find that we are often living in a mildly hijacked or stressed condition due to countless negative stimuli around us.

4. *Enhancing Emotional Intelligence*

As illustrated in Figure 3.7, we can improve our emotional intelligence by concentrating on three key components: Self-Control, Self-Regulation, and Self-Motivation.

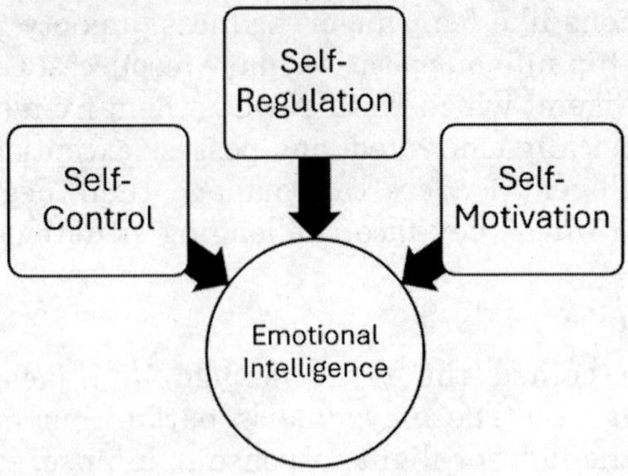

FIGURE 3.7 Key Components for Developing Emotional Intelligence.

I. Self-Control

Leaders who excel in emotional self-control remain calm and composed during stressful situations. They can think clearly in challenging circumstances, and their IQ and the executive functioning of the neocortex stay unaffected. To improve our emotional self-control, we should practice the following techniques:

(a) ***Self-Awareness:*** The most challenging time is not when no one understands us; it is when we do not understand ourselves. To connect with our emotions, the first thing we need is to become self-aware. We should recognize our instincts, our core beliefs, our passions, and the unique talents we possess. According to Nadler, "Awareness Equals Responsibility." Responsibility involves our capacity to respond positively in all situations or to account for our erratic behavior. We need to explore our inner landscape and gain insight into our strengths and weaknesses, mood fluctuations, changing feelings, common behavioral patterns in our daily lives, our impact on others, and our personal narratives. A refusal to examine our inner selves not only diminishes our motivation but also undermines our ability to inspire others through positive interactions. Reflecting on the following questions and reviewing the same questions and answers three times a day will enhance our self-awareness:

- What are my strengths?
- What are my weaknesses?
- Do I have frequent mood swings?
- How consistent is my behavior?
- How much do people trust me?
- What are my skills?
- How competent am I?

(b) ***Conduct an Emotional Audit:*** Whenever we encounter extreme adverse situations or face intense negative environmental stimuli, we are immediately charged with negative emotions, as fear and anger serve as our primary defenses against challenging circumstances. The emotional audit is designed to pose strategic questions that shift our focus from the emotional brain to the rational brain. The emotional audit questions and their responses help refocus the activity away from the emotional brain, redirecting blood and oxygen flow from the amygdala to our rational brain (PFC) and enhancing our cognitive control. The types of emotional audit questions are as follows:

- What am I feeling?
- What am I thinking?
- What is my real objective?
- What do I want now?
- How can I do it my way?
- What do I need to do differently?

(c) ***Affect Labeling:*** Psychology Professor Matthew Lieberman coined the term 'affect labeling,' which refers to the process of naming the emotions we feel in intense situations. Through this technique, rather than distancing ourselves from intense negative emotions, we approach them by experiencing, identifying, and naming them. Does this technique help us regulate our intense emotions? To test the effectiveness of this method, scientists conducted brain scans using an fMRI machine, where participants were shown photos displaying strong, frightening emotions. The brain signals revealed increased activity in the amygdala region, which is responsible for the fight-or-flight response. When these participants were asked to name the emotion, their brain signals showed a decrease in activity in the amygdala and an increase in activity in the right frontal lobe, specifically in the right ventrolateral prefrontal cortex (rvlPFC). The right ventrolateral prefrontal cortex is linked to vigilance and discrimination.

Alternatively, when the same people were asked to identify the gender shown in the picture, their brain signals did not reflect any decrease in activity in the amygdala. This experiment suggests that labeling the emotion we are experiencing causes our blood and oxygen flow to shift toward the frontal lobe of our brain, which is responsible for thought. Simultaneously, this reduces activity in the amygdala, decreasing the intensity of strong negative emotions. Therefore, whenever we encounter a challenging situation or intense negative emotion, we should begin to reflect on it by asking, 'What am I feeling right now?'

and we should articulate the emotion by saying, 'I think I am getting angry,' 'I think I am feeling fear,' or 'I think I am a little frightened right now.' By doing this, we can learn to manage our intense emotions and cultivate our emotional self-control.

(d) ***Reappraisal:*** Reappraisal is a psychotherapeutic technique that facilitates cognitive restructuring, allowing us to assign new, different, and more constructive meanings to our negative situations or experiences. This process helps redirect the flow of blood and oxygen to the prefrontal cortex. Reappraising a situation or experience can mitigate the effects of an amygdala hijack. We should ask and consider the following questions:

- What can I learn from this?
- How can I make this a meaningful experience for myself?
- What are two or three alternative interpretations that could be more accurate?
- What is the best course of action for me to take at this time?

II. Self-Regulation

Self-control techniques quickly alleviate an emotionally charged state of mind and restore normal thinking. In contrast, self-regulation techniques involve consistent practices to maintain a positive mindset in daily life.

A self-regulated individual demonstrates a higher emotional quotient and the ability to maintain a positive mindset in daily life. Self-regulation involves monitoring and managing our thoughts and behaviors in socially acceptable ways that lead to positive outcomes, such as favorable emotions, improved relationships, and personal growth. It also includes replacing negative habits, undesirable personality traits, negative attitudes, and perceptual distortions with productive and positive alternatives. Here are several techniques for self-regulation:

(a) ***Develop Internal Locus of Control:*** Julian B. Rotter introduced the concept of internal locus of control in 1954. Locus of control refers to the degree to which we believe we have control over the outcomes in our lives. Individuals with an internal locus of control view themselves as responsible for their life outcomes. In contrast, those with an external locus of control attribute their failures to outside factors.

Figure 3.8 illustrates two circles relevant to our lives: internal strength and external concerns. It emphasizes where we direct our attention. An external focus encourages us to consider how our surroundings affect our lives. In contrast, with an internal focus, we perceive it as centering on how I treat the people and situations around me, and thankfully, I treat them well.

FIGURE 3.8 Two Circles of Life.

What do successful people do differently? They possess an internal locus of control, believing they are responsible for their own destiny, whether it is positive or negative. They do not blame others for their failures and take responsibility for their actions; they wisely choose their attitude toward everything they encounter. They choose to be excellent, wealthy, and content. For individuals with an internal locus of control, there is no uncertainty in the outcomes of their lives.

Outcomes and actions are interconnected. An outcome emerges from the moment we first choose an action. Individuals with an internal focus base their decisions on their preferences. Their language is filled with phrases like, "I can be more patient, I can be more competent, I can be more knowledgeable, I can be more helpful to others," and so forth.

"No splendid has ever been achieved except by those who dared believe that something inside of them was superior to circumstances."
—Bruce Barton

The essence of our lives revolves around how much our presence impacts this planet. When we exercise an internal locus of control for our actions, we give purpose and meaning to our lives. We go beyond our visible capabilities to make a difference in this world. It also shifts our perception of life – "Life itself has no inherent meaning; we must provide meaning to our lives. We have not received life; rather, life has found us to make itself meaningful." Frankl strongly believed that the primary sources of our sadness, depression, anger, and frustration are the absence of meaning in our lives. It is our failure to attribute meaning or purpose to our existence. When we assign meaning or a significant purpose to our lives, we experience true happiness and joy. This is the principle of Logotherapy presented by Viktor Frankl.

In August 1997, when Stephen Covey, the renowned author of "The 7 Habits of Highly Effective People," learned that Viktor Frankl had lost his eyesight, was seriously ill, and was hospitalized, he visited the hospital to express his gratitude for Viktor's life's work. After graciously listening to Stephen's words of appreciation, Viktor replied, "Stephen, your words are making me feel like I am ready to check out, but I still have two projects to finish, and I will do it." Stephen could sense Viktor's remarkable integrity through his principle of Logotherapy. Viktor passed away in September 1997.

(b) ***Develop a Positive Attitude:*** Attitude is our subjective evaluation of any situation, person, or object, regardless of whether we view it as positive or negative. A negative attitude significantly affects our lives, trapping us in a state of constant stress. Our negative attitudes notably influence our relationships, health, happiness, well-being, and work. Factors such as worry, low self-esteem, low self-efficacy, anxiety, depression, fear, anger, and both physical and mental stress contribute to these negative attitudes, creating a reciprocal relationship.

Our negative thoughts are among the most significant sources of negative emotions. They arise from our limiting beliefs and perceptions, conditioning us to think in specific ways. For instance, when we face a new, challenging task at work, these limiting beliefs and negative perceptions can lead us to view the task as extremely difficult, if not impossible. We might think, "I lack the skills. Why was this task assigned to me instead of someone else? Why am I always singled out? What will happen if I fail to complete it?" These thoughts accumulate and contribute to a negative attitude toward the task.

If our limiting beliefs and perceptions are programmed to emphasize the negatives, it becomes challenging for us to shift our perspective. Our beliefs are not always accurate; they develop from our perceived experiences, which can often be misleading.

One of the greatest gifts that nature has given us is the ability to choose our attitude toward various circumstances. Choosing to be positive determines the richness of our lives. Our skills and abilities are important for success, but we cannot go very far without a positive attitude. If our attitude is negative, our life will be limited.

A positive attitude enables us to view even the most challenging situations as opportunities for hope. It effectively lowers our stress and helps us cope with difficult circumstances, fostering optimism and happiness. The adversity or appeal of a situation is not as critical to our success or failure; what truly matters is our attitude toward it. We cannot pretend to smile for long unless we genuinely desire to serve. If we smile sincerely at life, life will smile back at us. Almost all business organizations hire people for their skills but let go of those with a bad attitude because they recognize the significance of attitude in generating extraordinary performance results. Several techniques are available to cultivate a positive attitude, and a few key ones are listed below:

- *Be a Part of the Solution:* In any problem or situation, we should focus on being part of the solution. Solutions are inherently positive, while problems are inherently negative. The moment we start thinking about solutions, we immediately become positive and constructive individuals. We should always seek opportunities to add value to others' lives.
- *Eliminate all Negatives:* Upon observing our surroundings, we find that many negative people are present in our lives. These individuals may be our friends, relatives, colleagues, neighbors, or even enemies. We should identify the negative influences around us and work to remove them from our lives. We ought to free ourselves from their hold on our minds. These negative individuals constantly complain about everything, preventing us from seeing things from a positive perspective. Here, we must be cautious and distinguish between negative voices and those that offer constructive criticism. While constructive criticism may seem negative, it is rooted in positive intentions.
- *Live Your Vision:* One effective way to cultivate a positive attitude is by practicing living in the present. A robust method for achieving this is to embody our vision. Our vision provides us with a clear mental picture of our successful future, outlining how competent, knowledgeable, and wealthy we are. Instead of waiting for that mental image to become a physical reality, we should start embodying that future image in the present moment. We must feel as though everything is happening right now, and we should act like the healthiest, wealthiest, and happiest people we aspire to be.
- *Face Criticism:* We must recognize that no one is perfect in this world. We should view criticism as a blessing and an opportunity to learn. However, it takes a strong character to accept criticism. Ordinary individuals often shy away from criticism, ensuring they remain average their entire lives. We should believe that whatever situation we are currently facing is precisely the right one for learning. We must extract valuable lessons from every challenge and setback in life.

(c) ***Self-Observation:***

"It is not possible to engage in an unhealthy behavior while we are fully conscious about it." —*Bill Harris.*

We often believe we know ourselves, yet we do not realize that we are programmed machines. Self-observation is the most effective method for changing our neural pathways and eliminating undesirable emotional responses.

Typically, we rely on willpower to compel ourselves to change negative emotional reactions into positive ones. This forced approach can lead to neurosis. In contrast, self-observation acts as a passive technique for modifying our undesirable emotional responses. This method allows us to avoid making forceful attempts to control our habits.

Self-observation encourages us to closely watch all the consequences as we engage in the harmful habit of reacting aggressively to unwanted stimuli. These consequences may appear in our emotional state, physical condition, thought processes, people's reactions, performance outcomes, and the status of our interpersonal relationships.

This technique enables us to continue our habitual actions while silently observing everything that occurs. As observers, we should watch and document every detail while engaging in the behaviors we wish to change. For instance, when we feel angry, we shouldn't simply go out and try desperately to suppress our anger or become overly soft; instead, we should utilize the self-observation principle. When we experience anger, the self-observation principle recommends that we quietly watch ourselves in that state. We should objectively notice the types of thoughts arising in our minds, the emotions that are erupting, how those thoughts and emotions affect our behavior, what's happening around us, what types of consequences stem from our anger, and how others are reacting to our behavior. We should aim to observe the entire anger process.

If we engage in this repeatedly, there will come a time when we can create a new center within our neural web that recognizes our unwanted behaviors and their consequences. This new center will automatically establish fresh neural pathways for thoughts, emotions, and behavior patterns, allowing us to be no longer controlled by our anger.

Similarly, when we experience misery or despair, we should not try to escape our feelings, nor should we strive to be artificially happy. Instead, we ought to closely observe our feelings of despair or misery. We need to pay attention to the thoughts that arise and how others interact with us. With repeated observations, a time will come when we no longer feel misery or despair because our mind's neural network will understand how we create these feelings.

If we harbor fear, such as anxiety about future failure, we should not focus on how to eliminate these anxieties. Instead of trying to banish fear and anxiety regarding future failures, we should observe various occurrences, such as negative thoughts and feelings, declines in performance, people's reactions, and the state of our interpersonal relationships influenced by this anxiety. With consistent observation over time, the issue will be self-corrected by our subconscious, and we will no longer experience fear or anxiety about future failures.

Now, the question arises: What happens in our minds during self-observation? What is the neurobiological basis for this auto-correction?

Since our brains are vast networks of neural pathways without a central command, these neural networks aim to maintain the status quo and homeostasis. This is why any forced or neurotic attempts to change established behavior patterns or the status quo often result in self-damaging patterns.

Due to the power of our consciousness, we believe we are distinct from our neural hardwiring and that we can change it at will. However, we are not separate from the neural web that generates our consciousness; we are merely a part of the same neural web. Thus, any forced attempt to alter our neural wiring independently will lead to further complications, such as the release of excess stress neurochemicals. We should not even consider using moral self-teaching statements like "smoking is bad," "I should not smoke," "anger is not good," "I should control my anger," or "I should not drink alcohol; it is bad for my health." Attempting to change our habits with these moral statements is as ineffective as trying to exert seamless control over our neural wiring. It resembles micromanaging our conscious and subconscious processes.

While attempting to micromanage our neural web by forcibly suppressing anger, anxiety, fear, guilt, or any negative habits, we expend a tremendous amount of energy keeping our mouths shut and our faces expressionless. In this suppression process, we overwork a part of the brain known as the ventrolateral prefrontal cortex (VLPFC), which acts as a brake on emotional outbursts. Each time we suppress our emotions and behaviors, the VLPFC becomes weaker, much like the brakes in a car. Excessive use of suppression techniques can lead to the complete failure of the VLPFC, resulting in the loss of conscious control over emotional outbursts.

Self-observation is a technique that does not require extraordinary efforts to change our neural wiring. We need to communicate various occurrences, including thoughts, emotions, actions, and consequences, to our neural network through our observations.

It is similar to creating another center or a new neural seed within the existing neural web in our minds. When we repeatedly inform our brains of the same observations, the newly formed neural wiring becomes a neural hardwiring, and our neural web naturally begins to restructure itself around this new hardwiring without disturbing homeostasis. Isn't that a fantastic technique?

(d) ***Dilute Your Ego:*** One of the primary sources of psychological stress is our heavy-weight ego. The ego functions in our mind as our attorney, defending all our actions, whether good or bad. In the process of consistently defending ourselves and concealing our weaknesses, our ego compels us to act as if we are 'Mr. Perfect' or 'Miss Perfect,' with no flaws at all. Our ego is constantly concerned about the following:

- How do we appear to others?
- What are others saying about us?
- What will people think if they learn what we are really like?
- How will they feel about us then?
- How will they respond to us?
- What would happen to our social image?

Due to these perceived threats, we begin to lie to others and adapt to our ego pretensions. These ego pretensions compel us to pose or pretend that we are different from who we truly are. In this process of concealing and deceiving others, we generate a never-ending hidden stress in our minds.

Due to our ego, we identify ourselves through the lenses of our possessions, social status, position, education, knowledge, family, nation, race, or religion. These lenses do not represent our true selves; rather, they are mere pretensions intended to satisfy our ego. When we operate from our ego, we become judgmental and obsessed with right or wrong. This behavior separates us from our present reality and true self, trapping us in a downward spiral of rumination within our minds.

When we become truly aware of our ego, let go of it, and begin to operate from our true self, we become more transparent, altruistic, and passionate about serving others. In other words, we grow more compassionate. Our lives become more peaceful and loving. We stop controlling others and start seeing things as they are. Emotionally self-regulated individuals do not allow their ego to dictate their interpretations, decisions, and actions.

Here are some effective behavioral techniques we can practice to let go of our ego:

- **Accept Yourself and be Transparent:** By accepting ourselves as we are and becoming transparent, we build resilience. We become flexible like water, which can absorb many things, change its shape according to its container, and adopt any color. It is incredibly important for us to fall in love with ourselves. There is nothing wrong with us; we are all products of the exact mother nature. We are exceptional human beings, each with unique talents. Once we assure ourselves that we are doing the right things, we should not worry about what others think of us.

  At the same time, we should not place too much importance on ourselves because nobody else does. Once we become transparent, speak the truth, and accept ourselves with both our strengths and weaknesses, our self-esteem is significantly enhanced. Another benefit of being transparent and authentic is the social endorsement we receive from others, which further boosts our self-esteem. As our self-esteem increases, our psychological responses to various stimuli naturally become more positive. Our tendency to imagine negative future scenarios will decrease considerably. This will also enhance our ability to take risks.
- *Become Impersonal:* Stop taking things personally. Our ego loves to take offense and derives pleasure from pain. When people say something negative about us or our actions, they are prisoners of their conditioned minds. They feel compelled to speak because that is their role. We should give them the benefit of the doubt regarding their distorted perceptions or poor understanding. Let us not waste our energy on ego battles.
- *Forgive Others:* Forgiving others gives us a sense of freedom. It frees us from the burden of needing to be correct. Our ego fiercely defends us against being wrong. Forgiving others enables us to put our past behind us and embark on a fresh start.
- *Forget Social Validation:* Our ego craves love and social validation. It constantly seeks to be correct, to be seen and heard, and to win ego battles. Once we release our ego's need for social validation, we move toward our higher self, which does not expect anything from others. Our higher self aims to connect with people by spreading love, peace, and happiness. Embodying our higher self, we become aware of our ego's demands. According to Eckhart Tolle's research article published in the Harvard Business Review,

the moment we recognize our ego, it becomes an obsolete mental pattern, as awareness and ego cannot coexist.

(e) ***Heighten Your Self-Esteem:***

"No one can make us feel inferior without our permission."- Eleanor Roosevelt.

Self-esteem is the sense of self-worth. It reflects how we feel about ourselves. We all have an internal voice that informs us of our importance and value in the world. Our childhood experiences, along with the influences of parents, teachers, peers, neighbors, and relatives, play a significant role in shaping our foundational self-esteem. If these influences are negative and disparaging, our self-esteem may remain anchored at an unusually low level.

All our past experiences remain vivid as an inner voice in our subconscious. This inner voice continually reminds us of our worth. For those with high or positive self-esteem, the messages from this inner voice are encouraging and affirming. Conversely, for individuals with low or negative self-esteem, this inner voice shifts into harsh criticism and punishment. For those with low self-esteem, even a minor negative stimulus can generate significant stress, leading to anxiety, loneliness, and depression.

To enhance our self-esteem, we should begin by challenging the voice of our inner critic. To counter the negative messages from this critic, take a moment to write down at least five statements that highlight our positive strengths, past achievements, and joyful moments. Make sure to read these statements several times a day. Here are some examples that can help boost our self-esteem:

- I have the strength to face life's uncertainties.
- I possess the knowledge, skills, and abilities necessary to overcome any challenge in life.
- I genuinely deserve to be a successful person in life.
- I can manage my emotions effectively during stressful situations.
- I am eager to learn new skills, regardless of my age.

III. Self-Motivation

While leaders are expected to inspire and motivate their subordinates, who is responsible for motivating the leaders? Leaders must employ self-motivational techniques to inspire themselves. Self-motivation is the ability to pursue our desires without being influenced by others or our circumstances. It drives us to consistently work toward our life goals, even in challenging or adverse situations. Several important techniques can significantly enhance self-motivation.

(a) ***Have faith:*** Faith is taking the first step when we do not see the whole staircase. (Martin Luther King Jr.)

Faith is a powerful tool that can bring our desired reality into existence from nothing. To achieve success, we must have faith in that success. Faith represents a strong belief in the unseen and the invisible, which will ultimately be revealed in the future. It gives us complete assurance of our success in life. Faith is not merely about wishing or hoping for something to happen; it is about firmly believing that something good will occur. It encompasses our obligation, commitment, confidence, trust, devotion, conviction, loyalty, promise, and total surrender to universal consciousness.

Faith enhances our resilience in the face of struggles. Often, it is our lack of confidence in ourselves that makes us hesitant to confront challenges. When we cultivate faith, our worries diminish. Fear and faith cannot coexist; we must choose between believing that something good will happen and succumbing to the fear of failure. We should not allow our fears to overshadow our faith. In fact, fear is simply a form of faith in failure. It is our strong faith that empowers us to take the first step into the unknown. Faith is not merely hope; it serves as a guarantee of success.

Mr. Napoleon Hill, the renowned author of the bestseller Think and Grow Rich, emphasized that faith is an incredibly powerful emotion. He described faith as the "head chemist" of the mind. When faith is combined with positive thoughts, the subconscious mind picks up on these vibrations, translates them into a spiritual equivalent, and transmits them to cosmic intelligence to create a positive reality, whether related to health or wealth.

Faith is the only means through which we can harness and utilize the force of cosmic intelligence. It serves as the foundation for all miracles and mysteries that cannot be explained by the principles of Newtonian science. Faith is the starting point for the accumulation of desired realities and is the only antidote for all failures.

(b) ***Practice Gratitude:***

"Even in the midst of the greatest difficulties we experience in life, we can always find things for which we are truly grateful."

—Brian Tracy

The most powerful force in the universe is gratitude. It is the secret to a fulfilling life. Gratitude is the feeling of being blessed, opening the doors to endless possibilities. Rather than focusing on what we lack, it teaches us to appreciate what we have and to express thanks for it. By practicing gratitude, we can repair and rebuild our most strained interpersonal relationships. According to the Oxford Dictionary, gratitude is defined as "the quality or condition of being thankful; the appreciation of an inclination to return kindness."

Many of us often overlook the importance of what we already have in life, focusing instead on what we lack. This mindset can lead to a cycle of ungratefulness that prevents us from receiving more. However, when we express gratitude for our current blessings, we quickly discover even more reasons to be thankful. By radiating feelings of gratitude, we can experience immediate happiness in the present moment.

Gratitude is essential for nurturing a sense of happiness and abundance in our lives. When we express appreciation for our current circumstances, we open ourselves to receiving even more blessings that enhance our feelings of thankfulness. It is important to cultivate a daily habit of reflecting on everything we have. By doing so, we may uncover just how much there is to appreciate.

We can truly appreciate the beauty of each moment in our lives by being thankful for what life has given us. It is essential for us to decide right now to let go of blame, accusations, gossip, and complaints. We have only this one beautiful life, and we should learn to cherish every moment of it. The universe will provide us with even more to love. Regularly practicing gratitude for the wonderful things we have and expressing appreciation for the good things we have yet to receive can significantly contribute to our success in life.

To cultivate gratitude, we should embrace the "AA" formula, which stands for Attention and Appreciation. It's important to pay attention to the small, positive things happening in our lives. Focusing on gratitude means noticing and fully receiving the positive aspects around us. Often, we overlook many good things due to inattention, which prevents us from experiencing them to the fullest.

While we are taught the importance of giving to others, we often overlook the significance of receiving. This oversight can lead us to neglect the positive experiences that regularly occur in our lives. We should make an effort to listen attentively to those around us—our family, neighbors, and colleagues. Active listening is one of the highest forms of gratitude we can show to others. Additionally, we should recognize and appreciate the good behavior and deeds of those around us.

We should pay close attention to detail and take every opportunity each day to thank those around us for their contributions. A simple "thank you" is not enough; it should be accompanied by appreciation for every accomplishment, no matter how small. We must acknowledge every good effort, idea, or suggestion. Consistently compliment people on their qualities, such as punctuality, persistence, honesty, and sincerity.

We should express our gratitude not only for what we currently have but also for what we hope to receive in the future. It's essential to give thanks even before we witness positive outcomes. Can we truly feel grateful and experience the uplifting emotions linked to a desired future event, even before it happens? From the perspective of quantum creation, we must be thankful for the possibilities that exist in the quantum field but have not yet manifested in our physical reality.

(c) ***Set 10X Goals:*** Grant Cardone is the author of the bestseller "The 10X Rule," which emphasizes that to achieve significant success in life, we must elevate our thinking and actions to a level that is ten times greater than our current mindset and efforts. Cardone explains that it requires the same amount of energy and effort to earn $10 million as it does to earn $10,000. This illustrates that setting average goals leads to average outcomes, even if we apply the same level of effort that we would use for extraordinary goals.

Csikszentmihalyi is well known for his theory of the Flow Experience. He introduced the concept of the "Flow Experience," which suggests that it is a state of enduring gratification that occurs when we become fully engaged in an activity, to the point that we forget about other concerns, such as hunger and the passage of time. We often become so absorbed in an activity that nothing else seems to matter. A flow experience occurs when we engage in a task that presents a significant challenge and requires considerable effort. Therefore, dedicating extra effort to achieve ambitious 10X goals can lead to a flow experience.

The concept of 10X goals creates a significant amount of psychological energy and liberates us from the frustration of lacking the necessary education, talent, skills, or resources. The 10X rule suggests that any goal can be achieved with the right amount of effort and persistence.

Success is not just an option for us; it is a duty that we must fulfill, no matter what it takes. Ultimately, setting 10X goals instills in us a sense of purpose, making us feel as if we are destined to dominate the world. We must adopt the following formula to keep ourselves motivated 24/7:

10X Goals × 10X Efforts × 10X Persistence

(d) ***Never Give Up Mindset***

"There is no failure unless we quit."

Life is full of uncertainties, and there are times when we may feel stuck and frustrated because nothing seems to be happening. In these vulnerable moments, it can be tempting to give up, as quitting may seem like the easiest option. However, when we choose to quit, we often settle for far less than we truly deserve. So, why do so many of us prefer to give up in tough situations? The answer lies in the absence of a "Never Give Up" mindset, which requires us to train our minds to persevere and not quit under any circumstances. To develop this never-give-up mindset, we need to gain clarity on the following concepts:

- When we become overly focused on activities that satisfy our immediate desires, we quickly lose the motivation to put in consistent effort. If we do not genuinely love what we are doing, quitting becomes inevitable. Our passion for our pursuits provides the willpower needed to endure even the most challenging times in our lives. Therefore, we should strive to cultivate a strong passion for leading others.
- We often encounter setbacks while pursuing our passions. During these times, it can feel like we lack the strength to stand up again, making it seem as though giving up is the only option. However, whenever life brings us down, we must find the resilience to rise again. Many people face challenges, but do not fight back. It takes courage, confidence, strong willpower, and a determined mindset to recover, especially when no one else believes in us. We need to be highly motivated to achieve our vision and be willing to do whatever it takes.
- From childhood onwards, people never tire of telling us that we cannot do this, we do not have the resources, we lack the required skills, and our situation is different. We must reject all these demotivating voices and allow ourselves to come out of our shells and announce to everyone that we have emerged; we are born to conquer our dreams; we are destined to rule our lives; we are meant to follow our own path.
- Pessimists will urge us to be realistic, and naysayers may tell us to give up, but we must remember that it's our dream. No one will chase it for us, hunt for it, or support us. We must pursue it, no matter what. Our dreams can become a reality if we persist under extreme conditions. We should not stop chasing our passion until we achieve it.
- We should not let irrelevant voices persuade us that our goal is unattainable. It may be out of reach for pessimists or those who have failed, but it is certainly within reach for achievers like us. Do we want to pursue our dreams or live in fear and frustration?
- If we are waiting for something to change or for an event to occur on its own, we must recognize that nothing will change and nothing will happen unless we take action

ourselves. Improvement is not possible without our effort to advance. We have only one life, and it is indeed brief, so whatever we wish to achieve, we must pursue it now. The journey may be incredibly challenging, but it is not impossible. We need to show our character, and in time, people will remember us as the winners, the champions—the ones who never give up, the ones who fought back, and the ones who fought with passion.

- We cannot grow without struggle. We cannot develop strength without resistance and the challenge of pushing ourselves. Agony is our friend- maybe not in this moment, but it contributes to long-term results and strengthens our courage. Our strength, courage, and willpower stem from our disappointments, failures, and struggles. If we persist and grow under extremely challenging conditions, the world will fall in love with us.
- Who do we want to be: a coward or a combative person? A coward always settles for a life he does not want to live. A combative person is willing to give everything to achieve what he deserves. If we were to achieve every success right now without working for it, we would not feel fulfilled because we have not earned it. If we want to experience the pride of victory and understand what it feels like to be a champion, we must earn it. We should be willing to work hard for success. To reach the top, we must push ourselves through the pain. It's never about the prize or the money; it's all about the pride. We are warriors, not survivors.
- We have not covered this distance; we just need to reach here! We have reached here to become strong enough to go farther and farther. There is no end, and there is no destiny of success; it's always a journey of success, and wherever we are, it is just a beginning. We are proud of our success, but we are not going to settle for it. Please do not tell us it's over. We are just getting warmed up. We are unstoppable! We believe in ourselves even if we have no reason to believe. At our unsuccessful moments, we build our character and regain our strength to start all over again.
- We are not afraid of anything. Why should we fear something that has not happened and may never occur? Fear is a false assumption that feels real to our perception. It is merely an imaginary concept, just an illusion of negative possibilities. It's not our bad luck or adverse circumstances; it's our fear, the number one killer of our passion. It is the primary reason behind our failures. Fear is a voice inside us urging us to quit. It grows louder and larger whenever we listen to it. Fear is the voice of a loser or a settler. We must confront

our fear and eliminate it immediately. Fear must die. We must decide that we will not allow our fear to determine our destiny. We are far greater than our fear, and we will continue to overcome it until it is gone.

3.2.2 Communication Skills

Leaders are responsible for guiding their teams by aligning them with a shared vision, inspiring and motivating them, nurturing their potential, and resolving their conflicts. Strong communication skills are a pivotal and essential tool for effectively carrying out these leadership functions. Therefore, if we aspire to become great leaders, it is crucial to develop exceptional communication abilities. Figure 3.9 illustrates the key components of a leader's communication skills: reflective listening, persuasive communication, effective body language, and positive interactions.

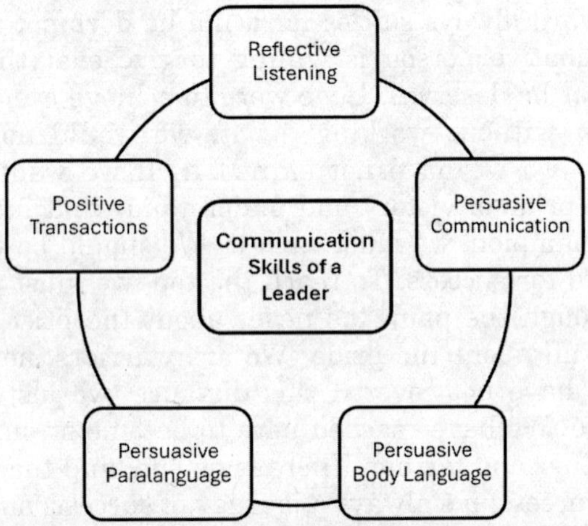

FIGURE 3.9 Components of Communication Skills of a Leader.

1. *Reflective Listening*

Listening is a crucial component of communication skills that requires adequate practice for a leader to master. Great leaders do not just hear what people say; they listen reflectively to gain a clear understanding and validate the true meaning of the communication. Reflective listening involves actively engaging with the speaker by paraphrasing, summarizing, mirroring emotions, and asking questions to clarify any ambiguity. In paraphrasing, the listener restates the message in their own words to gain better clarity. In summary, the listener emphasizes the key points to understand the overall message. In mirroring emotions, the listener made eye contact with the speaker and demonstrated empathy to comprehend the speaker's feelings. Reflective listeners pose open-ended questions to clarify ambiguity and enhance understanding. Asking open-ended questions is an important skill that encourages thoughtful responses from the speaker. Unlike yes or no questions, open-ended questions require more elaborate answers and often start with words like what, how, why, or describe. These types of questions help leaders promote discussion, gather more detailed information, and gain a better understanding of the speaker's thoughts, feelings, and overall state of mind. We can understand open-ended questions by reviewing examples of closed-ended and open-ended questions. A close-ended question is: "Did you finish the task?" This question can be answered with either "Yes" or "No." The open-ended question is: "Why do you think teamwork is important in the workplace?" This question encourages reasoning and explanation.

Example of Reflective Listening

Speaker: I am really frustrated with my manager because he works very haphazardly and always disturbs my schedules and routines.

Reflective Listener: It seems you are disappointed with your manager due to his chaotic work style. Can you elaborate on how this affects your routine work?

Leaders practicing reflective listening can provide confidence to their people that they are heard and understood by their leader. At the same time, leaders can diagnose core issues, hidden motives, and desires of their people.

2. *Persuasive Communication*

Persuasive communication is the process of conveying information in a way that influences the receivers' attitudes, beliefs, and motivations. The message is carefully crafted and delivered to appeal to logic, emotion, and credibility. Leadership communication involves top-down (leadership-to-employees) and bottom-up (employees-to-leadership) communications.

In a leadership-to-employee communication scenario, the flow of information typically moves from leaders to employees on the office floor. Leaders with strong persuasive communication skills can effectively convey their vision and inspire their teams while empathizing with their thoughts, feelings, and expectations. Leadership involves the use of persuasion to motivate and guide employees within an organization. Effective communication from leaders boosts employee morale and engagement and facilitates organizational change.

Effective communication is crucial for engaging employees in the communication scenario from employees to leaders. It promotes transparency, encourages individuals to share their thoughts and ideas, and makes them feel valued and connected to the company. As a result, this can lead to increased job satisfaction and productivity.

Three Pillars of Persuasive Communication

The three major components of persuasive Communication are ethos, pathos, and logos, which were first introduced by the ancient Greek philosopher Aristotle. These have become fundamental concepts in rhetoric and persuasion. These three pillars represent various strategies that writers or speakers can use to appeal to and convince their audience. Let us delve deeper into each pillar to gain a better understanding.

(a) **Ethos:** Ethos refers to the credibility or ethical appeal of a speaker. It involves establishing trust, credibility, and expertise to persuade the audience that the speaker is knowledgeable, reliable, and trustworthy. Ethos can be developed through various means, such as:

- Demonstrating expertise and knowledge in the subject matter.
- Highlighting relevant qualifications, achievements, or credentials.
- Establishing common ground with the audience.
- Displaying fairness, honesty, and integrity.
- By employing ethos, speakers or writers aim to gain the audience's respect and trust, which enhances their persuasive power.

(b) **Pathos:** Pathos is a rhetorical technique designed to evoke emotions in the audience. Its primary goal is to establish a strong emotional connection by appealing to their feelings, values, desires, and beliefs.

The effective use of pathos can significantly influence the audience's attitudes, opinions, and actions. Speakers strive to connect with their audience on an emotional level by appealing to pathos, which makes their message more relatable and persuasive. When making decisions, people often rely on emotions rather than logic. Skilled persuaders understand this and leverage it to their advantage. They adjust their tone and arguments according to the audience's emotional state.

(c) **Logos:** Logos refers to the use of logical reasoning to support an argument. It involves presenting well-supported, logical points backed by evidence, facts, and reasoning. The goal of logos is to persuade the audience through rational thinking and appeal to their intellect.

Some techniques used to strengthen logos include:

- Providing factual evidence, statistics, and research findings.
- Presenting logical reasoning.
- Anticipating counterarguments and addressing them effectively.

Using logos in communication aims to demonstrate the strength of arguments by appealing to the audience's logic and reasoning abilities.

Leaders often combine ethos, pathos, and logos to create a persuasive message, adapting their approach to suit the specific audience, context, and purpose of their message. Effectively combining these three pillars helps create a well-rounded persuasive appeal that can influence and persuade others more effectively.

3. *Persuasive Body Language*

Persuasive body language is a powerful tool for enhancing communication and influencing. Here are some tips for using persuasive body language effectively.

(a) **Eye Expressions:** Eye expressions play a vital role in non-verbal communication, conveying a wide range of emotions, intentions, and social cues. Often called the "windows to the soul," the eyes can reveal a person's feelings and emotions. Various emotions, such as happiness, sadness, anger, and surprise, can be communicated through eye expressions. Understanding and interpreting these expressions can enhance communication skills and lead to more effective and empathetic interactions in both social and professional settings.

(b) **Eye Contact:** Good eye contact is essential in both interpersonal and professional settings, as it plays a significant role in persuading others. It helps to create a sense of connection and rapport between individuals. By maintaining eye contact, we convey interest and engagement in the conversation, making others feel acknowledged and respected.

Good eye contact also demonstrates active listening. It shows that we are focused on the speaker and genuinely interested in what they have to say, which can lead to better understanding and more meaningful conversations. Additionally, eye contact can convey emotions, intentions, and attitudes, adding depth to our communication. This allows others to pick up on subtle signals and gain a clearer understanding of our message.

Sustained eye contact signifies confidence and sincerity; however, it's important to avoid staring, as it can come across as aggressive. Instead, we should strive for a friendly and confident gaze.

(c) **Facial Expressions:** Facial expressions are a primary way to convey emotions. Facial expressions such as smiles, frowns, and raised eyebrows assist in conveying our feelings and reactions to different situations. Facial expressions complement verbal communication by adding depth and nuance to our messages. A smile while delivering good news or a furrowed brow when expressing concern can enhance the meaning of our words. Use expressive facial expressions to convey enthusiasm, empathy, and sincerity. Expressive faces can foster connections with others. A warm and friendly expression can make people feel more comfortable and receptive to engaging with us. Maintaining a calm and composed facial expression can help diffuse tension during conflicts or disagreements, signaling a willingness to engage in constructive dialogue rather than escalate the situation.

A genuine smile is a powerful tool for connecting with others and creating a welcoming environment. We must ensure that our facial expressions align with our verbal messages. It is important to maintain consistency between our verbal and nonverbal communication. When our facial expressions match our words, it adds credibility to our message. Consistency between verbal and nonverbal cues enhances the clarity and authenticity of our communication. Remember that while effective facial expressions are important, they should be genuine and contextually appropriate. Being overly expressive or displaying inconsistent facial cues can lead to misunderstandings.

(d) **Posture:** Posture refers to the way we hold our body while moving, sitting, or standing. Standing or sitting straight with our shoulders back, head held up, and chin at 90 degrees to the neck reflects our confidence.

Posture is a non-verbal form of communication that can reinforce the assertiveness of our message. A confident and assertive posture can complement our verbal arguments, making our persuasive efforts more impactful. Good posture conveys confidence and credibility. Standing or sitting up straight gives the impression that we are self-assured and knowledgeable about the topic at hand. This, in turn, enhances our persuasive influence on the audience. Adopting open and expansive postures can have a positive impact by making us appear more approachable and powerful.

(e) **Gestures:** According to Britannica, a gesture is a movement of our hands that shows or emphasizes an idea or a feeling. Using purposeful hand gestures can help emphasize viewpoints and maintain audience engagement during presentations. This will help us to communicate our message and maintain our audience's attention effectively.

Gestures allow speakers to convey emotions and passion effectively. Appropriate facial expressions and hand movements can add depth to the emotional tone of the message, fostering a stronger connection with the audience. To effectively communicate our message, it is essential to avoid excessive or distracting hand movements, as they can diminish the impact of our message.

(f) **Handshake:** A firm handshake demonstrates confidence and strength. It should neither be too weak nor too strong, and the duration must be appropriate.

(g) **Proximity:** The concept of proximity refers to the physical or psychological closeness between the communicator and the audience. It is crucial to be mindful of personal space. Invading someone's personal space can lead to discomfort. Cultural norms influence the appropriate levels of proximity. Understanding and adapting to these norms is crucial for effective communication, as violating personal space boundaries can lead to discomfort and resistance. We should adjust our proximity based on cultural norms and the nature of our relationship with the individual.

(h) **Nodding:** Nodding in agreement demonstrates active listening and engagement. Avoid excessive nodding, as it may seem insincere or distracting.

(i) **Personal Attire:** The way we present ourselves, including our clothing choices and grooming habits, can significantly impact how others perceive us and the persuasive message we convey. Dressing appropriately for the occasion and demonstrating professionalism can enhance our credibility and create a positive impression. To be persuasive in our interpersonal communication, we must always keep the following in mind:

- Focus on good grooming, encompassing a tidy hairstyle, personal hygiene, polished shoes, and clean nails.
- Invest in professional-looking clothing and accessories.
- Avoid flashy garments, chunky jewelry, garish makeup, and overpowering perfumes.
- Make sure we feel comfortable in our attire.

It is important to remember that the impact of body language can differ depending on the culture. Therefore, it is essential to be aware of cultural differences when utilizing these techniques. Moreover, authenticity plays a crucial role in the effectiveness of nonverbal communication, also known as body language. Genuine and natural gestures are more persuasive than contrived or forced ones.

(j) **Body Odor:** Maintaining good personal hygiene, including avoiding unpleasant body odor, contributes to an individual's professionalism. A well-groomed appearance, proper body hygiene, and a pleasant fragrance can positively influence how others perceive us, potentially making our communication more persuasive and compelling. We should use appropriate deodorant to ensure a pleasant body odor. This practice fosters a more comfortable environment for communication, enabling individuals to focus on the message being conveyed.

4. *Persuasive Paralanguage*

Paralanguage refers to all vocally produced sounds that are not direct forms of linguistic communication. Voice conveys something beyond language. The way we speak, including tone, pitch, volume, and rhythm, contributes to the persuasive impact of our message. A confident, persuasive tone can convey authority and enthusiasm. Adjusting the voice to emphasize certain words or phrases helps draw attention and adds emphasis. Paralanguage acts as a powerful complement to verbal communication, enriching the persuasive process by adding emotional depth, emphasis, and credibility to the spoken message. Here are some important aspects of paralanguage:

(a) **Tone:** The tone of our voice can convey emotions and attitudes that may not be explicitly expressed through words. It adds emotional depth to a message, making it more compelling and relatable. The tone can be harsh, loud, gentle, or pleasant. We should maintain a soft, gentle, and pleasant tone when communicating orally with others.

(b) **Voice Modulation:** Voice modulation refers to the way we adjust the volume and speed of our spoken words to emphasize specific keywords. Variations in pitch, volume, and emphasis can highlight key points in a persuasive message. This helps in ensuring that the listener understands and remembers the most crucial elements of the argument. We should be mindful of how we use volume, pitch, stress, stretch, and pauses while speaking.

(c) **Articulation:** Articulation refers to the way we pronounce words using our tongue, jaw, teeth, and lips. The clarity of our spoken words can greatly influence others.

(d) **Tempo:** Refers to the rate at which someone speaks. If a person speaks too slowly, the audience will likely lose interest. Speaking too quickly leads to lower credibility. Therefore, A speaker should use an optimal rate to keep the audience interested and show confident knowledge of the subject. Speaking at an appropriate speed allows listeners to better grasp complex or unfamiliar information. This can be beneficial in educational settings, presentations, or when discussing intricate topics. Changing the tempo throughout a speech can help highlight important points. Dynamic and varied tempos can capture and maintain the audience's attention. Speaking at a consistently slow or fast pace may lead to monotony, making it harder for listeners to stay engaged.

Mastering the art of tempo control can enhance persuasive communication. For instance, slowing down during a persuasive argument conveys confidence and thoughtfulness, while a quicker tempo expresses enthusiasm.

In storytelling, a dynamic tempo can bring narratives to life. Slower pacing during critical moments builds suspense, while faster pacing signifies action or excitement.

(e) **Dysfluency:** Dysfluency refers to any interruption in fluent speech. One must learn to deliver fluent speech. Fluent speakers can convey their thoughts and ideas clearly, reducing the risk of misunderstandings. It allows individuals to articulate their emotions and opinions effectively, enhancing the impact of their communication. Fluent speakers can collaborate more efficiently by clearly communicating their ideas and perspectives, resulting in more effective problem-solving outcomes.

5. *Positive Transactions*

In his theory of transactional analysis, Eric Berne proposed that our actions, thoughts, and spoken words are all transactions, significantly influenced by the experiences we accumulate from childhood to adulthood. A transaction is defined as a unit of social interaction consisting of two components: the transactional stimulus and the transactional response.

When two people interact, one person may communicate using spoken words, body language, or actions, which we can refer to as a transactional stimulus. The other person then responds to this stimulus through verbal replies, actions, facial expressions, body posture, or gestures, which is known as a transactional response.

As a leader, our interactions with followers, colleagues, and other stakeholders are crucial for developing positive interpersonal relationships. If we take the time to reflect on our spoken words in daily conversations, we may realize that we often unintentionally hurt others with harsh comments. Phrases like "You do not know anything," "Do not talk to me," "It is your problem, not mine," "You are useless," "You cannot do anything," "Just do what I say," "I will see you," "You stand nowhere in front of me," "Know your place," "Keep your mouth shut," "Get out of my room," "Get lost," "Go to hell," "Be ready to face the consequences," "You do not know me," and "I will show you who I am" can damage relationships and create a hostile atmosphere. It is important to communicate with positive transactions to foster a healthy and productive environment.

On the other hand, our positive transactions could include phrases such as: "I appreciate your knowledge," "You are so kind," "Thank you for your help," "I value your advice," "I would like to have further discussions with you on this topic," "You are very competent," "It was really nice talking to you," "I hope to see you soon," "Please take care of yourself," and "Do not hesitate to ask me if you need anything." These positive interactions can help build productive relationships with people and foster desired performance within the organization.

3.2.3 Compassion

Great leaders have a profound sense of compassion. Compassion is the ability to feel sympathy for the suffering of others, which enhances our desire to help them. When we are compassionate, we empathize with the pain of others, which makes us more altruistic and rational in our actions.

To be compassionate, we must empathize with others. Compassion extends beyond mere empathy or loving-kindness, although both are essential components. In addition to empathy, compassion includes a genuine desire to help others during their vulnerable moments. Empathy occurs when we experience somatic, affective, or cognitive resonance with someone who is suffering. It can be described as a fusion of the other person's state of being with our own. Additionally, it may be seen as an expansion of our own state of being. According to Dr. Joan Halifax Roshi, compassion is our capacity to attend to the experiences of others.

As per Buddhist philosophy, compassion means the ability to see the world for what it is, rather than our judgment of what we make of it. Therefore, we reflect compassion when we describe people or situations without being judgmental or getting involved emotionally. We should always be willing to help everyone around us.

On the contrary, while being compassionate towards others, we should be able to distinguish ourselves from them. If we consistently and deeply delve into another person's suffering and continue to empathize without practicing self-care, we risk experiencing empathic distress. According to the Dalai Lama, compassion requires a strong backbone and a gentle front, allowing others to approach us and touch our hearts while also enabling us to maintain our distinction and stand firmly to help them.

According to neuroscience, nothing is external, and all minds are connected with the help of mirror neurons; therefore, the way we look at the world, the world looks at us in the same way. Great leaders instantly connect with their subordinates' minds and spread peace and happiness by being compassionate.

3.2.4 Creating Synergy

Effective leaders foster synergy in their relationships with others. Synergy arises when two individuals or groups achieve exceptional results that they could not accomplish alone. It stresses mutual trust, transparent communication, and creative compromise to enhance innovation, productivity, and problem-solving abilities. Leaders cultivate a culture of mutual trust and transparent communication, allowing team members to feel safe taking risks and sharing ideas. Figure 3.10 demonstrates that when mutual trust and transparent communication are strong among individuals or groups, creative compromise emerges, leading to synergy where performance results surpass the combined capacity of the individuals.

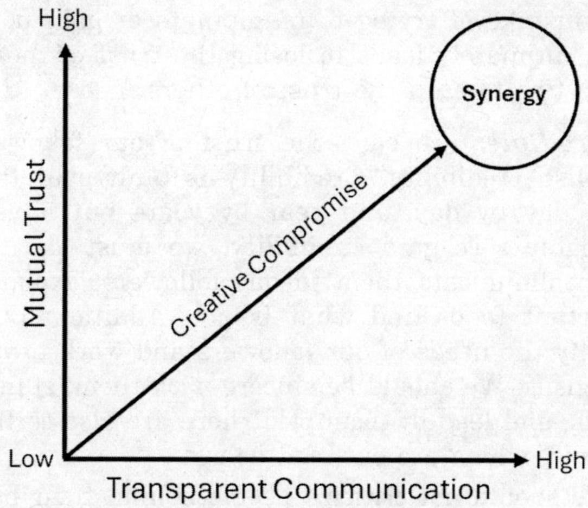

FIGURE 3.10 Synergistic Relationship.

1. *Mutual Trust*

Building trust with others takes a significant amount of time and effort, and losing that trust can happen in an instant. Regaining someone's trust after it has been lost is often the most challenging task. True relationships rely on mutual trust, which serves as the emotional glue that binds leaders and their followers together. When trust is absent, it leads to stress, communication barriers, lack of cooperation, suspicion, and decreased productivity in the workplace. Therefore, one of a leader's primary responsibilities is to cultivate a trustworthy environment. This mutual trust establishes a foundation for synergy, fostering true interdependence and deep respect among individuals.

In our leadership training programs, most participants ask how to build trust and foster trustworthiness in others. They also wonder if there is a way to assess the trustworthiness of their team members. Many participants expressed that they trusted their colleagues, but when those same individuals betrayed that trust, they felt uncertain about where they went wrong.

The answers to these questions hinge on two key concepts: "become" and "trustworthy." As leaders, it is our responsibility to be trustworthy for our team. We must take the initiative; we cannot expect others to be trustworthy if we do not embody that quality ourselves. To earn trust, we need to be believable, credible, and truthful with our team first; only then can we reasonably expect them to be trustworthy in return.

Be sure that if people trust us, they are trustworthy, and if they do not trust us, they are not. Trust involves telling the truth, but it goes beyond merely avoiding lies. It also includes presenting the truth in a way that minimizes the potential for misinterpretation. Many of us make the mistake of trying to manipulate or gain power from the system, which ultimately leads to losing the trust of those around us. Here are some tips to earn the trust of others:

(a) ***Be credible:*** To earn the trust of our followers, we must establish credibility. Credibility is built over time—hour by hour, day by day, and year by year—but it can be lost in an instant. To gain credibility, we must clarify our values and communicate them to our followers, explaining what is important to us and what is not. Additionally, we need to identify the needs of our followers and work towards building consensus. We should be sincere with them, stand firm in our beliefs, and lead by example. There are also certain behaviors to avoid, which are outlined below:

- We should not criticize people behind their backs.
- We should not let others down during their vulnerable moments.
- We should not hurt someone's feelings. Remember, "An injury is forgiven more easily than an insult."
- We should avoid using our position or authority to manipulate relationships.
- We must opt for face-to-face interactions instead of requesting written explanations.
- We should not simply say "yes" to maintain a good image; learn to say "no" when necessary.
- We should focus on being the right person rather than trying to be nice.

(b) ***Be Courteous:*** Courteous individuals are simple and grounded. They do not hurt others' emotions and respect differences. They appreciate other viewpoints even if they do not agree with them. They are peacemakers; their presence brings harmony to the environment.

Consider the situation where we wanted to cross the road, but heavy traffic was preventing us from doing so. How did we feel when someone recognized our predicament, slowed down their vehicle, waved at us, and allowed us to cross the road? Definitely, our frustration would quickly turn into relief and gratitude.

Courtesy involves showing respect and kindness towards others. A courteous person, even if not exceptionally clever, will achieve greater success in life than a sharp but discourteous person. This quality greatly aids in winning the hearts and trust of others.

How can we practice courtesy? Throughout the day, we encounter many people, and each interaction presents an opportunity. Whenever someone treats us kindly, it's important to show our appreciation, express our gratitude, and offer sincere thanks. Additionally, we should give a genuine smile when meeting others. Remember, a smile is a simple and inexpensive gesture that can resolve many issues.

We should acknowledge the achievements of others with sincere and heartfelt praise rather than superficial flattery. It's important to respect the opinions and decisions of others, even if we disagree with them. Being a good friend and treating everyone with respect, regardless of their position, is essential. When faced with rudeness, we should respond with kindness. We should never underestimate the power of our small acts of kindness; they serve as pebbles that form a solid foundation for our trustful relationships with people.

(c) ***Emotional Condensation:*** Emotional condensation refers to the emotional deposits we make in the hearts of others. When we do something good for people, keep our commitments, and perform small acts of kindness, we deposit positive emotions in their hearts.

If we scold people, shout at them, betray their commitment, and hurt their emotions through our misconduct, we actually withdraw emotions from their hearts. This is a continuous process in human interactions, and as a leader, we must always try to condense the emotional reservoir in people's hearts.

Regardless of how much we have helped someone in the past, if our emotional deposit is absent or negative due to our withdrawals, our relationship with that person will always be on the verge of breaking. To build our emotional reservoir in people's hearts, we must understand them, listen to them patiently and empathetically, be courteous, pay attention to the small details, keep our commitments, and help them passionately whenever they need it.

We should not underestimate the importance of sincerely apologizing whenever we make a withdrawal. Demonstrating integrity to our colleagues is also crucial. We must defend our team members when they are not present. By doing this, we can make significant emotional deposits not only in the hearts of those we are defending but also in the hearts of those present.

In interpersonal relationships, it's essential to clarify each other's expectations. We typically observe that individuals in relationships start to expect more and more without communicating, which leads to unfulfilled expectations. At this point, the process of emotional withdrawal begins, and emotional reserves drop to the breaking point or even lower.

(d) ***Respect each Other's Beliefs:*** Everyone has unique belief systems and perceptions shaped by their culture, religion, society, social groups, and families. People often attempt to impose their beliefs, lifestyles, and perspectives on others, expecting them to respect and adopt the same views. This tendency is a significant source of differences and a lack of trust between various religions and communities worldwide. It is essential for us to be open-minded and to distance ourselves from our cultural, regional, and religious biases. By doing so, we can genuinely appreciate the beliefs of others and cultivate the wisdom to discern what is good and what is not.

(e) ***Be Affectionate:*** Affection is often seen as the essential glue that binds relationships together. Many people feel utterly isolated without it, while its presence nurtures strong emotional bonds. When a friend shows affection, it feels wonderful; however, a lack of affection can lead to feelings of distress, highlighting our emotional need for it. Affection embodies care and conveys crucial feelings of security, protection, comfort, and approval, all of which are vital components of any relationship. When one person expresses affection towards another, they communicate several meaningful messages:

- You are important to me.
- I will care for you and protect you.
- I am concerned about your problems and will be there for you whenever you need me.
- I need you because I love you.

Affection is an emotion that flows between people, characterized by both giving and receiving. It helps individuals uphold each other's dignity and is not limited to a simple exchange; rather, it often involves sacrificing for one another. To be affectionate, we must sometimes listen to our minds but always follow our hearts. We should ensure we look people in the eye and smile sincerely.

2. *Transparent Communication*

Transparent communication is openly and honestly sharing information in interpersonal situations. It fosters confidence, collaboration, and clarity in professional and personal relationships. In addition to openly and honestly sharing information, transparent communication includes active listening, timely updates, and constructive feedback. Individuals must listen actively to one another and must acknowledge and validate each other's concerns. People should provide timely updates about any changes in circumstances. Feedback should be provided in a respectful and helpful manner. It promotes open discussion about challenges and areas for improvement.

3. *Creative Compromise*

The principles of Creative Compromise suggest that two individuals or groups with differing interests or perspectives can find optimal solutions or outcomes. These optimal outcomes are not merely the middle ground but innovative solutions that maximize mutual benefits. There are two key aspects of creative compromise described below:

- **Cooperation over Bargaining:** Instead of bargaining with each other to compromise their desires and settle for discounted performance, individuals and parties should collaborate to leverage each other's strengths and fully meet everyone's needs.
- **Innovative Mindset:** People should be more flexible and open-minded to discover the best innovative solutions by exploring unconventional ideas. An innovative solution is not merely an average or compromise that necessitates each party to give something up; instead, it involves finding a better outcome for everyone that addresses their deeper needs and motivations.

ASSESSMENTS

1. Describe proactivity. Using suitable examples, explain Viktor Frankl's stimulus-response theory.
2. Differentiate between vertical and lateral thinking processes. How will you develop your lateral thinking ability?
3. What is emotional intelligence? How will you enhance your emotional intelligence?
4. With suitable examples, explain reflective listening.
5. What are the three pillars of persuasive communication? How will you use them to persuade your followers within the organization?

CHAPTER 4

Envisioning and Alignment

4.1 Leadership Functions

Leadership involves guiding individuals to implement significant organizational changes, enabling adaptation to a rapidly changing environment, and achieving the organization's vision, mission, and objectives. While this definition of leadership may seem straightforward, it can create the misconception that anyone in a managerial position can effectively perform leadership tasks. In reality, leadership is one of the most challenging roles within an organization. Research indicates that managers at all levels—frontline, middle, and top—spend 90 percent of their time resolving human conflicts, with only a 20 percent success rate. Thus, to successfully perform leadership tasks and achieve organizational goals, managers must execute various leadership functions with exceptional excellence. Figure 4.1 illustrates six important functions of leadership.

FIGURE 4.1 Leadership Functions.

4.2 Envisioning

Envisioning is the process of creating a mental image of a desired future, developing strategies to achieve that vision, and taking action to transform it into a tangible reality. This approach serves as the first step in organizational leadership. Any effort to fulfill a leadership role without a clear vision is likely to fail. One of our key responsibilities as a leader is to set a course for the future, align everyone in the organization with that vision, and motivate them to move in the same direction.

Employee motivation and energy are essential for the success of any organization. The role of leadership is to align everyone's energy towards a common goal. Many individuals who call themselves managers in the corporate world mistakenly believe that leadership is merely about building friendships with subordinates and persuading them to complete their tasks. In reality, this approach is more similar to salesmanship.

Real leaders inspire their employees by elevating their vision and guiding them to destinations they may never have imagined. Research shows that, on average, senior executives in today's organizations dedicate less than 3 percent of their energy to developing a long-term corporate vision, with some companies reporting figures as low as 1 percent. As a leader, it is essential to distance ourselves from focusing solely on immediate results or the day-to-day routine. Instead, we should explore future possibilities to set the right direction for the organization and align all stakeholders with it.

4.2.1 Power of Vision

A vision is a clear, distant picture of our organization or unit that provides direction and a sense of purpose. Every business starts with a vision fueled by the hope that what is merely an idea today can eventually become a reality.

Vision is a source of faith, optimism, courage, passion, inspiration, psychological energy, and perseverance. It allows us to see what is invisible and gives us the ability to achieve the impossible. The key principle of vision is never to think small; always think big, create grand ambitions, and strive to achieve great things in life. Vision empowers us to write a beautiful script and live an extraordinarily wonderful life.

A clear vision acts as a guide, steering the company in its chosen direction. It serves as a guiding star, drawing everyone in the organization along the same path toward the future. When a vision is authentic, individuals excel because they are motivated to do so. The practice of creating a shared vision involves the skill of uncovering the 'pictures of the future' that foster genuine commitment and engagement among employees.

Vision is not just about having a plan; it is about maintaining a mindset that continuously strategizes. As a leader, it is crucial to ensure that everyone in our organization or unit focuses on, understands, and is committed to achieving the vision.

Vision is a powerful tool for aligning people and uniting a diverse workforce. It provides a common direction for the organization's employees, simplifying thousands of detailed decisions. A clear vision energizes individuals and fosters their commitment. It liberates people from monotony and dullness by presenting them with challenges that are worthy of their best efforts.

A powerful vision enables an organization to achieve significant change by engaging its people's actions and efforts. It serves as a link between today and tomorrow, acting as a bridge to the future. This vision motivates individuals to take the right steps forward, even when those initial steps may be personally challenging. Ultimately, it reveals future possibilities in the present.

Ordinary people believe only in what is possible. Extraordinary people visualize not what is possible or probable but rather what is impossible. And by visualizing the impossible, they begin to see it as possible" (Cherie Carter–Scott 1999).

4.2.2 Important Characteristics of a Vision

1. **Vision must have mass appeal:** An ideal vision should represent the organization collectively rather than emphasizing a single leader or the top leadership team. It should align all employees towards a shared direction, making everyone a stakeholder in the organization. This allows each individual to act independently while still moving in the same direction.
2. **Imaginable and Desirable:** The message must clearly convey a vision of the future. It should align with the long-term interests of employees, customers, stakeholders, and all other parties invested in the organization. Additionally, it must evoke an emotional connection by addressing our fundamental needs and desires to feel valued, important, and capable of making a real difference in the world.
3. **Feasible, Flexible, and Communicable:** A vision should include realistic and attainable goals. It must be broad enough to encourage individual initiative and alternative responses to changing conditions. It should be expressed in clear and straightforward language so that it can be communicated and understood effectively. If we can't explain our vision to someone in five minutes and capture their interest, refining and developing our vision further is essential.

4.2.3 Envisioning Process

The following are the sequential steps involved in the envisioning process:

1. *Creating a Future Picture in Mind*

We must develop our ability to see the invisible. When creating a vision, we should avoid comparing our dreams to our current reality. The picture we create is not an accurate vision if it appears real. It should look unreal; otherwise, it will limit our potential. We must detach ourselves from our existing reality and focus on the organization's future possibilities.

2. *Write a Clear Description of the Vision*

The practice of summarizing a vision in one or two lines has become outdated. Instead, we should describe our vision in detail. It should be written in the present tense because, at a metaphysical level, the vision represents the current reality of the organization. Our subconscious mind does not recognize the concepts of the past or future; it only understands the present. We can transform our vision into a tangible reality only when our subconscious mind believes in it.

Our subconscious mind operates in an impersonal manner. If we see our vision as the future reality of the organization, our subconscious will start working toward that reality, although it may never manifest in our present. Writing about our vision in the present tense allows it to be perceived by the subconscious as a current reality.

When outlining our vision, we need to include specific details such as the sales revenue and profit percentage the organization aims to achieve in a particular financial year. We should also emphasize the quality of the products and services we provide to our customers, the level of customer satisfaction, the skills and competencies within our organization, and the richness of our resources. Furthermore, we must consider the satisfaction levels of our employees, as well as their expected financial security and social status.

3. *Develop Strategic Actions*

Action without vision is aimless, while vision without action is merely fantasy. An organizational strategy acts as our action plan, outlining innovative steps to bring our vision to life. Innovation is crucial because it showcases the uniqueness and effectiveness of our approach to achieving our goals.

It's time to outline all the strategies we've used in the past to achieve our vision. Remember, nothing is impossible, impractical, beyond our reach, or unattainable. We should approach this exercise with a sense of fun, as this will help generate a lot of energy and foster innovation in our approach.

This exercise will enhance our belief in our vision. First, we should list about 10 to 15 innovative strategies that align with our vision. After that, we need to choose the best combination of strategies for implementation. These strategies may include collaborations, partnerships, market development, new product development, diversification, differentiation, no-frills strategies, segmentation, positioning, low-cost strategies, premium products, and exceptional services, among others.

The best combination of strategies should be selected after a thorough analysis of our organization's strengths and weaknesses, available opportunities, potential market threats, and the nature of our business.

4. *Organize all Resources to Achieve Vision*

By effectively utilizing resources like personnel, machinery, finances, and materials, we can achieve our vision and elevate our business to new levels of success. On the other hand, inefficient use of these resources can lead to significant losses. It is essential to develop our human resources to meet performance expectations. Building strong teams and ensuring collaboration among all departments is crucial to realizing our vision.

4.3 Alignment

Research in quantum mechanics and neuroscience indicates that our destiny is shaped more by our identity than by our desires. This emphasizes the importance of ensuring that all employees are emotionally aligned with the organization's vision. When employees connect with that vision, they can begin to embody and actively pursue the desired future.

When everyone in a unit or organization starts to think and feel in harmony, their thoughts and emotions become synchronized. This alignment transforms the vision into tangible reality. All individuals involved with the organization will unite their minds, focusing on the organization's vision with laser-like precision. Consequently, success becomes inevitable.

How to Align Employees with Vision?

Aligning employees emotionally with our vision can be more challenging than it appears. At first, most employees are likely to resist and doubt our vision. They may view it as mere daydreaming or a fantasy that is unlikely to materialize. Since achieving emotional alignment with the organizational vision is crucial, it is important to utilize the theory of Emotional Transition to facilitate this process. According to the theory of emotional transition, employees in organizations typically are in any of the four emotional stages that leaders need to overcome and respond to. These stages are Denial, Resistance, Exploration, and Commitment, as illustrated in Figure 4.2.

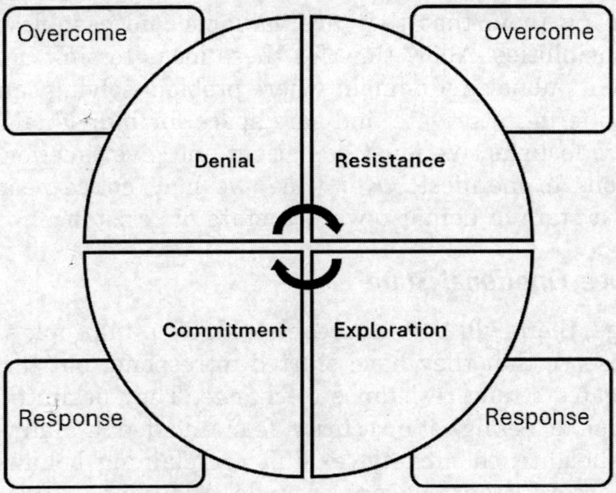

FIGURE 4.2 Emotional Transition.

1. *Denial Emotional State*

When employees encounter incompetence, high levels of demotivation, dissatisfaction, and low self-esteem, they often enter a state of denial. At this point, they lose interest and enthusiasm for their work and may express attitudes such as "I don't care" or "I'm not involved." These employees become rigid and resistant to changes, whether in the workplace or in their personal routines. They show little concern for the organization and its challenges, and they are highly sensitive to any changes that occur. Ultimately, they are unwilling to step outside their comfort zones.

How to Overcome Denial?

To overcome denial, present the current state of the organization and reassure them that change is on the way. We should share comprehensive information about our vision and instill a sense of urgency. Our enduring passion and tireless efforts toward our vision can break the ice, helping to persuade those who are in denial. To effectively communicate our vision, it is crucial to consistently articulate it in both formal and informal interactions with our employees. Paint an appealing and inspiring picture in their minds. We must ensure that our behavior aligns with our vision and strategies. If there are moments when our actions seem inconsistent with our vision, take the time to explain those reasons in detail.

As a mentor, it's important to help individuals adjust to changes and clearly explain what they can expect from the new system. We should highlight the gaps between the organization's current state and its desired state and emphasize the benefits of the change.

Identify each person's hidden potential and communicate this to them, assuring them that they are valuable and capable of handling their responsibilities. Allow time for these ideas to sink in.

Create a public environment where problem-solving can take place while also offering a private and safe space for individuals to express any negative feelings. We must be patient and give time for the results of our actions to manifest. Over time, we may notice people start to move from a state of denial toward a state of resistance.

2. *Resistance Emotional State*

At this stage, there will be a noticeable reduction in people's numbness. We may observe that they have started to respond, but their negative mindset creates strong resistance to change. They hesitate to embrace new ideas due to feelings of insecurity, fear, and doubt. Many individuals experience heightened anxiety, exhibit complaining behavior, express anger, and are reluctant to speak or smile. Additionally, they may delay in completing tasks.

How to Overcome Resistance?

To overcome people's resistance, we must first earn their trust and listen carefully to their reactions. Create a safe environment where employees can express their concerns and negative feelings. Avoid personalizing their responses; instead, focus on understanding and acknowledging their emotions. Use empathy to connect with them effectively.

We should not dismiss or attempt to talk them out of their feelings. Instead, we should support them, cooperate with them as needed, and always be present for them. Inspire them by sharing the success stories of great individuals. Encourage them to ask as many questions as they want. Instill confidence in their abilities and promote their participation and involvement. We must assure them that we will take responsibility for any negative consequences. Celebrate small wins and give them full credit for their achievements.

3. *Exploration Emotional State*

This stage is characterized by people's willingness to perform, but they struggle to excel. The positive energy among individuals is clearly visible as they generate numerous ideas and questions. People are eager to achieve excellence and are excited to learn new techniques. However, those at this emotional stage often feel disorganized, confused, and indecisive, lacking a clear focus.

How to Respond to Exploration?

Now is the ideal time to emotionally connect our followers with our vision and encourage their commitment to it. We should organize various training programs to help individuals enhance their skills. As a mentor, it's important to clarify their priorities to prevent confusion. Additionally, we can conduct brainstorming and planning sessions that encourage them to develop strategies for achieving the vision. This approach will help them maintain focus. We should recognize their ideas and reward their initiatives while celebrating small wins along the way. Gradually, we can delegate responsibilities and empower them to make decisions.

4. *Commitment Emotional State*

Individuals in the commitment stage are organized, optimistic, goal-oriented, and focused. They are willing to take on new responsibilities and can achieve excellence in their endeavors. They work well with others and effectively implement actions. They are satisfied with their work environment and maintain a clear sense of direction. They understand their roles and are aware of management's expectations.

How to Respond to Commitment?

Now is the perfect time to implement the necessary strategies to achieve our vision. We should empower our dedicated employees by granting them the autonomy to make decisions and execute the strategies they have developed. It is essential to cultivate self-directed teams comprised of dedicated individuals. We need to think ahead and create reward systems to motivate them. Focus on intrinsic motivation by giving employees responsibilities and fully empowering them to make decisions while publicly recognizing their achievements. Additionally, we should establish an organizational structure that facilitates change and creates a support system to ensure effective performance.

How Alan Mulally Utilized Vision to Avoid Bankruptcy at Ford Motors?

When Alan Mulally became the CEO of Ford in 2006, the company was struggling, having lost $12.7 billion and teetering on the brink of bankruptcy. He had the option to declare bankruptcy and accept a bailout package from the U.S. government. However, he chose not to pursue the bailout. After careful analysis, he realized that employees lacked clear direction and their actions were not aligned with the company's objectives. Additionally, there were issues such as internal silos, poor communication, misaligned priorities among leadership, and low morale among employees.

Alan created a clear and simple vision for Ford Motor Company, which states that the 'One Ford' plan aims to work together to transform the company into a viable and exciting entity that delivers profitable growth for all. The key components of the 'One Ford' plan include 'One Team,' 'One Plan,' and 'One Goal' worldwide. With the 'One Ford' vision, Ford Motor achieved global brand consolidation, global product development, and financial stability. To align all employees with his vision, he first eliminated internal silos by stopping Ford's divisions from competing against each other. Alan promoted global collaboration on a standardized vehicle global platform.

He eliminated all unnecessary costs while ensuring job security for core employees. He organized leadership training programs for all managers, asking them to align their teams with the company's vision and long-term objectives. He developed a policy that rewards teamwork and problem-solving instead of individual competition. Additionally, he introduced "Weekly Business Plan Review" (BPR) meetings, where executives can discuss challenges and solutions without fear of punishment. The company returned to profitability in 2009, just three years after Alan's arrival.

ASSESSMENTS

1. Define Vision. What are the important characteristics of an organizational vision?
2. Create a vision for your organization or unit and write about it in a detailed manner.
3. How will you emotionally align your followers with your vision?

CHAPTER 5

Leading Change

5.1 Why Change?

If we believe that the methods we have used in the past, which have led us to success, are the only way to achieve future success, we may be hindering the growth of our organization. The future hinges entirely on our actions today. Success is determined by choice, not by chance. If we want to thrive, we must explore new paths rather than continue down the worn-out corridor of conventional success.

Keeping our organization stagnant is the fastest way to move backward in a rapidly changing world. As the saying goes, "Many believe they understand the situation, but what they fail to grasp is that it has just changed." In this fast-paced environment, those who cannot recognize the need for change, are unwilling to adapt, or are unable to evolve, are part of a lost generation.

The world is rapidly changing due to a shift from a unipolar to a multipolar world, a single reserve currency to a multi-currency basket, technological advancements, increased competition, the transfer of wealth from the global North to the global South, and evolving markets. These driving forces create threats for those who are unwilling to adapt while providing opportunities for organizations that embrace change.

If an organization does not actively pursue change, it can easily fall into complacency, resist necessary transformations, and ultimately face decline. Resisting change widens the gap between an organization's current state and its evolving environment. Over time, these change-resistant organizations invest a considerable amount of energy in denying the need for change, leading to stagnation instead of progress.

Figure 5.1 clearly illustrates that these organizations will eventually face a critical decision: either implement radical changes to their systems or confront inevitable decline. However, these radical changes may require significant energy and funding and may encounter

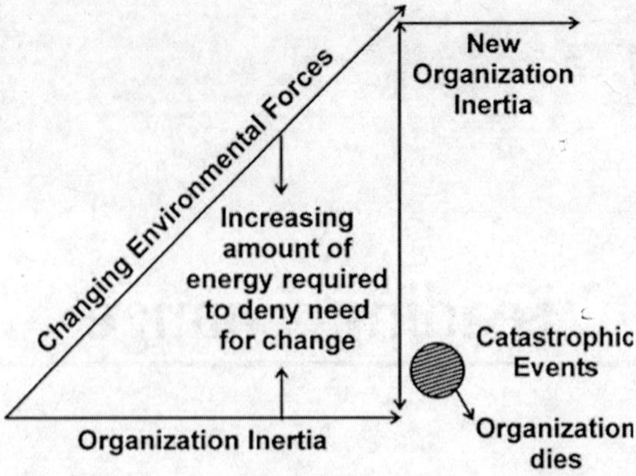

FIGURE 5.1 Destiny of Change Resistant Organization.

substantial resistance from employees, potentially leading to disastrous outcomes that could result in complete business failure.

Change-sensitive organizations view change as a continuous process and adapt to environmental changes, as illustrated in Figure 5.2. They make incremental adjustments in response to warning signals that indicate a need for change. By doing so, these organizations align themselves with their environment, making necessary modifications at regular intervals. This proactive approach allows them to require less energy to cope with environmental shifts.

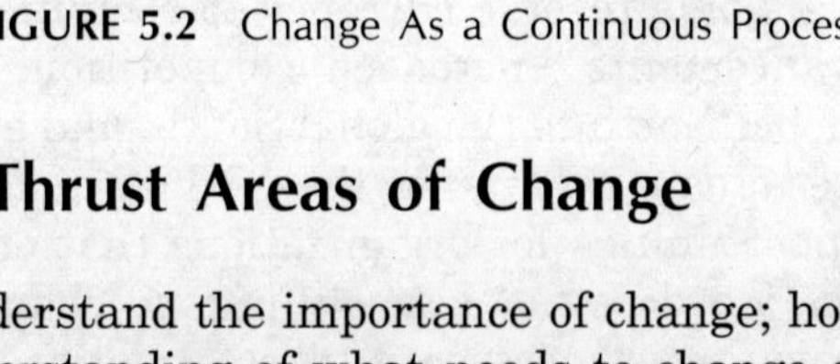

FIGURE 5.2 Change As a Continuous Process.

5.2 Major Thrust Areas of Change

Most leaders understand the importance of change; however, they often lack a clear understanding of what needs to change or which areas of the organization require improvement. Figure 5.3 identifies three major areas that should be regularly examined for necessary changes.

The first key aspect is the process, which refers to the procedures followed in business functions. As consumer needs, product preferences, buying patterns, market dynamics, lifestyles, government policies, and technological advancements evolve, these processes must be adjusted to provide customers with greater value at lower prices, offer premium products, ensure easy accessibility, and deliver better services. Regular

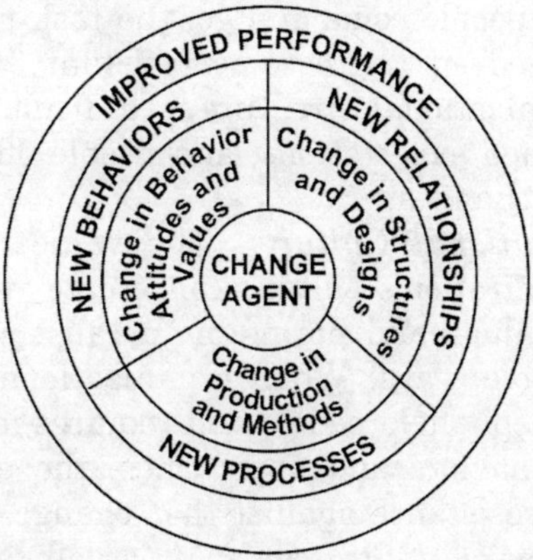

FIGURE 5.3 Major Thrust Areas of Change.

innovation and the development of new processes are essential to remain competitive in these areas.

The new structures and reporting relationships within an organization help prevent complacency and enhance productivity. Implementing these structural changes requires a cost-benefit analysis, a clear understanding of the authority and responsibilities associated with each position, and the appropriate span of control needed for effective management. Additionally, cultural analysis and transformation are essential for developing competencies and core capabilities within the organization.

Employee behavior and attitude also need improvement. A positive change in these areas can enhance how individuals function within the organization, how they engage with one another and with clients, the values they uphold and share, and their commitment to the organization's vision, mission, strategies, and objectives.

5.3 Resistance to Change

Various forces resist change within organizations. Broadly, these forces of resistance to change exist at three levels: the organizational level, the group level, and the individual level.

1. **Organizational-Level Resistance to Change:** The forces that resist change at the organizational level include the organizational structure, culture, strategy, and processes.
   - *Organizational Structure:* An organization's structure can hinder change. When a company establishes its organizational structure, it creates a stable pattern of task relationships that influence employee behavior. Over time, if this structure becomes self-sustaining—meaning that

even as people come and go, the task relationships remain unchanged—it can become resistant to change. Modifying an organizational structure is difficult because it disrupts established expectations, and people often react negatively to such changes.

- *Organizational Culture:* The values and norms within an organization's culture can create resistance to change. These values and norms often cause people to behave in predictable ways. When organizational change threatens these deeply held beliefs and requires individuals to modify their behaviors and approaches, the existing culture can lead to resistance against that change.
- *Organizational Strategy:* An organization's strategy can hinder change. Managers often cling to past commitments, continuing with a course of action even when it is no longer effective. Additionally, organizations may pursue strategies that were successful in the past but no longer create value.
- *Structuring of Processes:* Organizations sometimes adhere to well-structured processes that create structural inertia. These established procedures resist change, as they are designed to maintain stability.

2. **Group-Level Resistance to Change:** Groups establish their own norms to encourage desirable behaviors. Most members tend to conform to these norms, particularly in closely-knit groups. As a result, any changes that disrupt these established norms often provoke resistance from group members. Sometimes, groups resist changes that do not provide direct benefits to them individually. Additionally, the pressure to conform can prevent the group from considering alternative viewpoints.
3. **Individual-Level Resistance to Change**

   Cognitive Biases: People perceive the same situation in different ways. When changes occur, individuals often focus on how it will affect them personally instead of considering the broader implications for the whole organization.

   Lack of Information: People will resist change if they do not understand what is expected of them or why the change is necessary. When the reasons for change are not clearly communicated, individuals may fill in the gaps with their own assumptions, often assuming the worst about the initiator's intentions and their personal impact. Additionally, if people lack sufficient information on how to implement the change, they may fear making mistakes, which can prevent them from even attempting to adapt.

   Fear of the Unknown: People often resist change when they are unsure how it will impact their well-being. For instance, they might wonder how downsizing or a new online business-to-business marketing will affect their job security. Other concerns may include fears about their ability to perform well and the potential loss of positions, income, status, or power.

Habit: Breaking a habit is challenging because it requires effort and involves relinquishing perceived benefits associated with the habit, even when the new behavior offers more favorable outcomes.

Power Struggle: Change often benefits specific individuals and groups while harming others. When change leads to a power struggle, individuals will likely resist it.

5.4 How do Leaders Overcome Resistance to Change?

Strategic Leaders initiate change and disrupt the existing organizational paradigm; therefore, they are responsible for aligning the demands of a changing situation with the best strategies to overcome resistance while minimizing disruption. They overcome resistance to change, not through positional power but by leveraging trust and persuasive communication rooted in emotions, logic, and ethos. They are exceptional storytellers who captivate others with visions that shape the future in compelling ways. Leaders adopt the following practices to overcome the resistance to change.

1. **Education and Communication:** Leaders play a crucial role in helping people understand the reasons for a change, how it will be implemented, and the likely consequences. Even if the anticipated outcomes are generally positive, clear and extensive communication is essential to alleviate anxiety. This helps individuals grasp what is happening, what will be expected of them, and how they will be supported in adapting to the change.
2. **Participation and Involvement:** Leaders encourage everyone involved to help design and implement changes, which allows them to share their ideas and fosters commitment. Participating in the change process increases their understanding, enhances their sense of control, reduces uncertainty, and promotes a feeling of ownership, especially when the changes directly affect them. It is challenging for individuals to resist changes that they themselves played a role in creating.
3. **Facilitation and Support:** Leaders offer encouragement, support, training, counseling, and resources to help those impacted by change adapt to new requirements. By acknowledging individuals' anxiety as valid and assisting

them in coping with change, managers are more likely to earn respect and commitment, which enhances the chances of successfully implementing the changes.

4. **Negotiation and Agreement:** Leaders negotiate to provide incentives in exchange for an agreement to implement changes. This approach is often essential when facing strong resistance, such as from bargaining units. At times, specific items can be traded for support in facilitating change. In other instances, general perks can be distributed broadly, making it easier to accomplish the change.

5.5 The Change Process

The eight-stage change process is outlined here, based on the works of Kotter (1996) and Hambrick, Nadler, and Tushman (1997), to implement changes successfully within the organization.

Establish a Sense of Urgency

Change leaders must identify the challenges their organizations face by recognizing deficiencies, pinpointing sources of distress, and clearly outlining the negative consequences of inaction. Organizations must realize the necessity for change ahead of their competitors. This change requires a thorough evaluation of the external environment, including competitors and market forces, to accurately assess the current situation and identify potential threats and opportunities within the market. It's essential for the organization to evaluate the environment as a whole to determine the necessary changes rather than concentrating on just one factor.

Figure 5.4 illustrates Kurt Lewin's Force Field Analysis Model, which highlights two opposing forces that influence the change process within an organization. The driving forces push organizations to implement changes to adapt to environmental demands. In contrast, the restraining forces resist these changes, encouraging the organization to remain static. To initiate change, we must increase the factors that facilitate change while minimizing the impact of those who oppose it.

Assessing the consequences of avoiding change is essential. The benefits of change must outweigh those of maintaining the status quo. This thorough assessment is crucial for the organization's future sustainability and to help top management secure staff support by reducing complacency regarding the existing circumstances. Making people aware of the costs of failing to change for themselves and the organization is crucial.

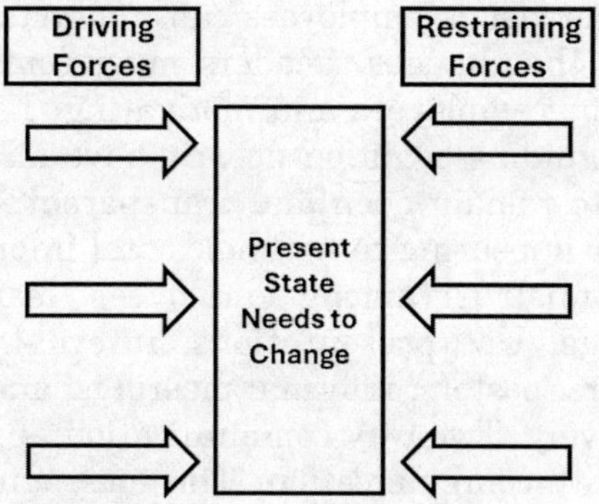

FIGURE 5.4 Force-Field Analysis.

Create Guiding Coalition

An individual alone cannot effectively lead a significant change initiative; a collaborative team of diverse members is essential. This team should consist of individuals with the right mix of skills, trust, and shared objectives. Four key characteristics of an effective team include positional power, expertise, credibility, and leadership. Leaders must build coalitions with influential organizational stakeholders to foster commitment and cooperation. Creating teams that include knowledgeable and credible individuals representing all levels of the organization is crucial. This approach will drive the change process and help ensure that established goals are achieved.

Develop a Vision and Strategy

Leaders must offer viable alternatives to the current situation through a clear and compelling vision that illustrates why it is the most appealing choice. Followers need to perceive the change program as realistic. A well-defined vision clarifies the direction of the change, motivates people to take action, and helps coordinate the efforts of various individuals. A compelling vision should be imaginative, desirable, feasible, focused, flexible, and easily communicable.

Clear communication about the current situation and the potential benefits of a change initiative is essential for an organization. This clarity helps individuals overcome their fears and resistance to change. A dynamic and focused approach is a powerful mechanism for driving change and continuous improvement. Maintaining continuity throughout the process is also essential, as individuals often feel anxious without something to hold on to.

Communicate the Change Vision

Clear communication of the vision is crucial for alleviating employees' fears and gaining support for the change process. When leaders effectively convey the vision, employees can understand their roles and the reasons behind the changes. Leaders must communicate honestly and directly, inspiring employees and motivating them to embrace the vision. Even if the guiding coalition doesn't have all the answers, it is essential for them to remain open and transparent.

Withholding or appearing to withhold vital information can create an atmosphere of mistrust among employees, leading to increased resistance to change. Use presentations, internal media, broadcast channels, call centers, posters, informal meetings, and memos to convey a new vision effectively. Two-way communication is more effective and preferable to one-way communication. The messaging should be kept clear and straightforward, avoiding technical jargon. Consistency in communication is essential, and the behavior of senior members of the organization should align with and support the vision.

Empower Broad-Based Action

Empowerment grants employees the responsibility, authority, and resources to take initiative independently. Significant internal transformation relies heavily on the support of employees. However, many employees often feel powerless to contribute due to various limiting factors. These factors may include rigid organizational structures, lacking essential skills or personnel, inadequate information systems that hinder action, and supervisors who discourage efforts to implement a new vision.

The organization's operating environment must be aligned with the vision for the necessary changes. Additionally, a plan should be developed to train current employees and, if required, we should recruit new staff. This will ensure that all personnel possess the necessary skills and talents to implement the new strategies effectively.

Generate Short-Term Wins

A short-term win refers to the recognition of specific goals that have been achieved during a change process. These wins are visible, clear, and closely tied to the change effort. In smaller companies, initial short-term wins are usually anticipated within six months. In contrast, larger organizations often aim for these wins within eighteen months. Short-term wins offer several advantages:

- They strengthen the change initiative by demonstrating that the sacrifices made were worthwhile.
- Positive feedback boosts morale and can enhance motivation.
- These successes can help the guiding coalition refine the change vision and strategies.
- Resistance to the change initiative diminishes.
- Visible results help secure and maintain management support.
- Short-term wins contribute to building momentum for the change initiative.

Consolidate Gains and Produce More Change

Organizations must be cautious about letting their sense of urgency for change diminish when celebrating short-term wins. This is a critical stage where there is a risk of reverting to former practices. Major changes, particularly in larger organizations, can take several years to fully implement.

Factors that can hinder the successful implementation of change include the turnover of key change agents, employee exhaustion, and unforeseen challenges. Ideally, this stage of the change process should be characterized by:

- Increased change, as the guiding coalition leverages the credibility gained from short-term successes to pursue larger change initiatives.
- More individuals are recruited and developed to support the change process.
- Senior management actively fulfills its leadership role and maintains a high level of urgency.
- Employees in lower ranks take on leadership and management roles for specific projects.
- Unnecessary interdependencies between departments are identified and eliminated, simplifying the change process.

Insert New Approaches into the Culture of the Organization

The final step in the transformation process depends on how effective and beneficial the new approaches are compared to the old ones. Often, it is necessary to change key individuals within an organization to shift its culture, as these individuals typically represent the existing culture. The "paradox of success" suggests that what drives success today can become the status quo for tomorrow. Consequently, transformational leaders must promote a culture of continuous change within their organizations. This involves fostering an environment that encourages employees to question established practices and rethink traditional ways of doing things.

How HubSpot Overcame Resistance to its Transition to a Freemium Model

HubSpot grew by selling high-priced software packages and became the leading company in the software sales industry. In 2015, the company faced intense challenges from competitors such as Salesforce and other startups. CEO Brian Halligan decided to implement the Freemium Business Model to stay competitive. This model allows customers to access the basic features of a software package for free while charging for premium services. However, this shift encountered significant resistance from company employees. Below are the concerns expressed by HubSpot employees:

- Salespeople were concerned that the freemium model would reduce paid subscriptions, which in turn could hurt their commissions.
- Employees were satisfied with the current pricing model and were reluctant to embrace the new model.
- Transitioning to a freemium model will necessitate extensive changes in technical, sales, and customer support processes.
- Investors believed that the Freemium Model would negatively impact the company's profitability.

How Brian Overcame Resistance

Brian conducted a cost-benefit analysis and compiled all the data, presenting it through graphs and charts. In his comprehensive report, he explained to the resistant employees and investors why the Freemium model is necessary. He highlighted how this model would attract a large number of users, increase conversions, and support long-term growth. He organized regular company-wide meetings and Q&A sessions, allowing employees to voice their concerns and receive reassurance from upper management.

Instead of implementing the model across the entire market, Brian tested it on a small scale. He redesigned the company's commission structure so that the sales team receives a bonus when users convert to paid subscriptions. He made changes to the technical, marketing, and customer support processes. When the company achieved small success, Brian used that data to convince employees and investors, leading to the large-scale implementation of the Freemium Model. HubSpot's Freemium Model became a tremendous success, increasing its revenue from $270 million in 2016 to $1.7 billion in 2023.

ASSESSMENTS

1. What are the major thrust areas of change in any organization?
2. Why do employees resist change within the organization, and how will you overcome their resistance to change?
3. With suitable examples, narrate the change process.

CHAPTER 6

Mentoring and Counseling

6.1 Mentoring

Mentorship is a process by which the skills, knowledge, values, and life experiences of a selected, successful manager are transmitted to another employee in the organizational system to grow that employee for greater efficiency and effectiveness (Nasser & Vivier, 1995).

Mentoring is a system of semi-structured guidance in which one person (the mentor) shares knowledge, skills, and experience with another person (the mentee). This relationship is characterized by authority and nurturing, with the mentor being more experienced than the mentee. Mentoring is an effective way to preserve and transfer corporate knowledge. It plays a crucial role in developing strong leaders, who, in turn, train future leaders. Ultimately, mentoring helps employees reach their full personal and professional potential.

Mentoring is an effective way to tailor career development to align with a corporation's mission and to foster a strong corporate culture. It significantly promotes employee commitment to organizational values, builds a high-performance culture, enhances competencies, and develops core skills.

A mentor is someone we trust to have our best interests at heart; they are willing to tell us what we need to know, even if it might be difficult for us to hear (Missirian, 1981). In this role, a transformational leader identifies the untapped potential within employees and the critical areas that require improvement. They provide personalized teaching and coaching to help employees fully develop their potential. Mentors align their mentees with the organization's vision and strategic goals, collaboratively setting personal objectives and creating action plans to achieve them. Ultimately, they inspire and offer emotional support to their mentees.

6.1.1 Mentor-Mentee Relationship

The relationship between a mentor and a mentee is similar to that between a parent and a child or between a teacher and a student. This dynamic operates within four dimensions, as illustrated in Figure 6.1 below. These dimensions include accepting, rejecting, undemanding, and controlling. The mentor-mentee relationships are categorized as follows:

Neglected mentoring arises from dimensions that are undemanding and rejecting. *Permissive mentoring* emerges from undemanding and accepting dimensions. *Authoritative mentoring* is characterized by accepting and controlling dimensions, while *authoritarian mentoring* is defined by controlling and rejecting dimensions.

1. *Neglected Mentoring Relationship*

A neglected mentoring relationship develops when mentors are not compassionate or emotionally connected to their mentees. Additionally, the mentor fails to make an effort to guide or manage the mentee's behavior, which is entirely undemanding. The outcomes of this type of relationship include employees' lack of alignment with the organizational vision, disciplinary issues, inadequate personal and professional development, and overall average organizational performance.

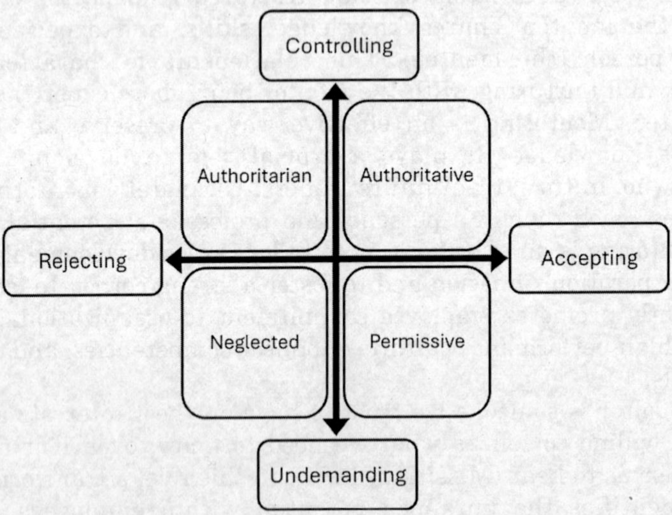

FIGURE 6.1 Mentor-Mentee Relationships.

2. *Authoritarian Mentoring Relationship*

An authoritarian mentoring relationship signifies a dictatorial attitude in which a mentor tries to control the mentees' behavior without getting emotionally attached to them. The nurturing component is missing; everything is imposed on mentees irrespective of their willingness or unwillingness.

Authoritarian mentoring is characterized by control and a lack of acceptance for mentees. Authoritarian mentors establish numerous rules and tend to micromanage, providing little warmth or emotional support. They offer minimal opportunities for negotiation and rarely allow mentees to make their own choices. These mentors do not engage in persuasion; instead, they simply instruct mentees to follow their directions. They do not focus on discussing feelings and typically refrain from praising good work, believing that recognition might encourage mentees to ask questions. Additionally, they are often quick to point out faults rather than provide constructive feedback.

While some decent performances may arise from induced fear, employee motivation remains extremely low. Workers guided by authoritarian leaders become anxious and lack self-discipline.

3. *Permissive Mentoring Relationship*

Permissive mentors are nurturing and affectionate. They accept their mentees and consistently strive to be kind to them. However, they often fail to enforce development plans, discipline, and rules, and promote self-regulation and self-control. This leniency can lead to the acceptance of inappropriate behavior from their mentees. They tend to act more like friends than maintain a professional mentor-mentee relationship. Their mentoring style is typically unstructured and includes inconsistent rules, emphasizing freedom rather than responsibility and accountability.

Employees who receive such mentoring show low achievement across various aspects. They make poor decisions, exhibit increased aggression, demonstrate limited emotional understanding, and struggle with productive time management.

4. *Authoritative Mentoring Relationship*

Authoritative mentors are loving, nurturing, and responsive. Yet, they expect their mentees to comply with plans, rules, and standards of self-discipline, self-regulation, and self-control. They are attentive to their mentees' emotional needs while maintaining high expectations. These mentors set clear limits and consistently enforce boundaries. They listen patiently to their mentees, allowing them to share their opinions, and they express warmth in their interactions.

Authoritative mentors take the time to address their subordinates' doubts and persuade them with strong, logical evidence. As a result, employees achieve extraordinary success in all areas of their lives. They demonstrate self-regulation, self-confidence, rational decision-making, emotional regulation, and self-discipline.

6.1.2 Mentoring Process

According to Stephen Covey, mentoring is not just about sharing knowledge and experience; it also involves effective teaching and coaching from mentors to their mentees. The mentoring process can be categorized into five sequential steps, as illustrated in Figure 6.2.

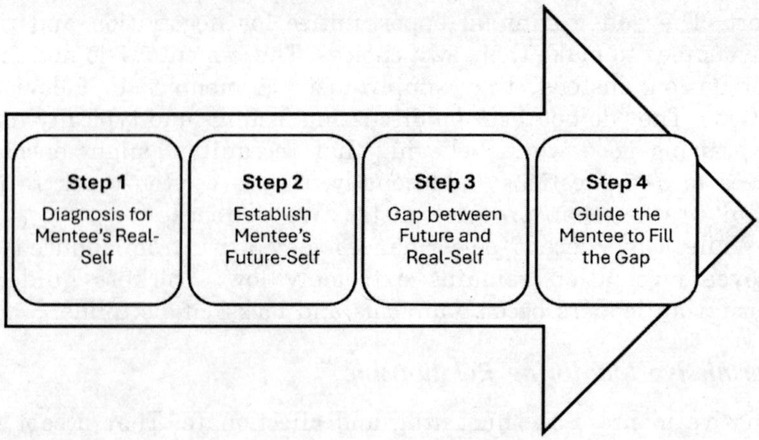

FIGURE 6.2 The Mentoring Process.

1. *Diagnosis*

At the diagnosis stage, mentors identify the mentee's real self or present state of being, which includes personal problems, untapped potential, hidden narratives, development needs, and aspirations.

Every human being possesses tremendous potential, though many are unaware of it. Albert Einstein once remarked, "I think I used about 25% of my intellectual capacity during my life." Similarly, psychologist William James noted in 1897 (republished in 1956) that humans typically utilize only 10 to 12% of their potential, leaving around 90% in a dormant state.

The saddest aspect of many people's lives is that they leave this world with their unexpressed music still inside them. By analyzing employees' strengths and weaknesses, mentors can identify areas for improvement and offer effective teaching and training to help them achieve their goals and objectives.

To identify the mentee's real self or present state of being, exceptional mentors utilize the Johari Window Model. This well-known framework for understanding interpersonal dynamics is based on two key parameters: self-disclosure and feedback. Developed by Joseph Luft and Harry Ingham, the term "Johari" is derived from the first few letters of their names. Figure 6.3 depicts four window types based on self-disclosure, feedback, and shared discovery mechanisms.

Self-disclosure refers to the information that mentees share about themselves with their mentors. This information can encompass a wide range of topics, including life experiences, personal circumstances, thoughts and feelings, likes and dislikes, habits, dreams, and opinions.

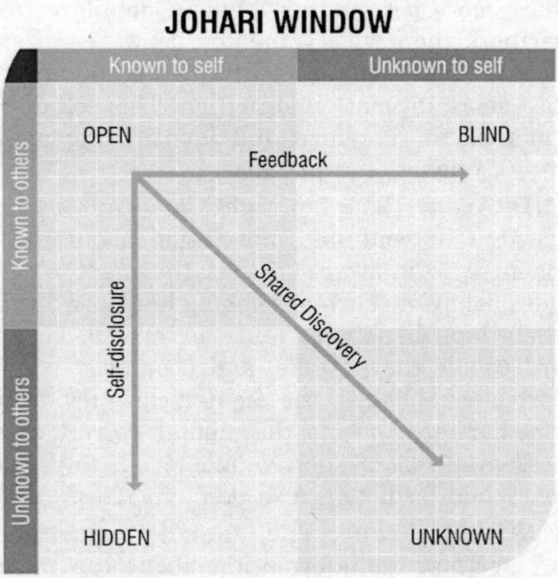

FIGURE 6.3 Johari Window Model.

The key aspect of self-disclosure is that the information shared with mentors should be honest, straightforward, and genuine. It is vital to avoid any form of ego or social pretension when disclosing this information. Showing only our best side does not constitute true self-disclosure. Mentees can discover their hidden potential, positive and negative habits, and unrecognized passions through feedback from their mentors.

The Johari Window model, illustrated in Figure 6.3 above, consists of four different quadrants involved in the interpersonal exchange of information.

(a) **OPEN Area:** The top left quadrant, known as the Open area, represents information that the mentee knows about themselves and is also apparent to others. It includes details such as the mentee's gender, skin color, age, knowledge, and skills—all of which are recognized by both the mentee and the mentor. The mentor can initiate and maintain a positive dialogue with the mentee by discussing this open area. This interaction allows the mentor to build rapport with the mentee.

(b) **HIDDEN Area:** The bottom left quadrant labeled "Hidden Area" contains information about the mentee, including their likes and dislikes, past experiences (good and bad), thoughts, feelings, and dreams. This information is known to the mentee but not to the mentor.

Individuals tend to be selective when it comes to sharing information with their mentors. For instance, they are likely to share more personal or "hidden" details with close friends or partners than with a mentor. However, a strong rapport between a mentee and a mentor can encourage the mentee to disclose more intimate information. This self-disclosure allows the mentor to recognize and identify the mentee's hidden potential, talents, and passions.

(c) **BLIND Area:** The top right quadrant is known as the Blind Area. It contains information about the mentee that the mentee is unaware of, but the mentor can observe. It includes behaviors such as rubbing hands or drumming fingers on their lap, displaying tense or erratic facial expressions toward people they dislike, and poor body language. Once a rapport is established, the mentor can provide both feedback and feedforward to help the mentee correct these behaviors. The essential role of effective mentors is to provide consistent feedback and feedforward to their mentees.

(d) **UNKNOWN Area:** The fourth quadrant, "Unknown Area," pertains to information about the mentee, such as their suppressed feelings, past negative experiences, hidden narratives, and undisclosed instincts or passions. This type of information is often called "unconscious material," meaning that neither the mentor nor the mentee has conscious access to it. Through ongoing dialogue, feedback, and self-disclosure, the mentor and mentee can explore this unknown area, read between the lines, and uncover hidden potential or personal challenges collaboratively. Discovering information from an unknown area is denoted as a shared discovery, which is a unique value proposition of the Johari Window Model.

2. *Establish the Mentee's Future-Self*

Using the Johari Window Model, mentors can gain insight into the mentee's real self, including personal issues, concealed narratives in the subconscious mind, hidden potentials, aspirations, and personality traits.

Now, it is time to establish the mentee's future self. As a mentor, we should first analyze the organizational objectives and then define our mentee's future self regarding the knowledge, skills, competencies, attitude, values, and personality attributes required to achieve the organizational vision, mission, and objectives.

3. *List the Gap between Future-Self and Real-Self*

At this stage, we understand our mentees' real and future selves. It is much easier to outline the gap between their current and required attributes for the future.

4. *Provide Guidance to Fill the Gap*

Once the gaps are fully identified, the next step involves mentors guiding mentees toward achieving their desired future selves. As mentors, we must work collaboratively with our mentees to create action plans. These plans may include on-the-job behavioral and technical practices, participating in classroom workshops and lectures, and taking on leadership roles and decision-making responsibilities.

6.1.3 Teaching and Coaching

Through effective teaching, we can inform employees about the organizational vision, business strategy, values, desired behaviors, products, services, and outcomes. We should consider our mentees as consumers of knowledge. Good teachers are flexible, fluid, experimenting, and have the confidence to adjust to changing circumstances. Effective teaching requires humor. It is often about making innocent and harmless jokes, mostly at our own expense, so that the barriers can be broken and employees learn in a more jubilant and relaxed atmosphere. It is about caring, nurturing, and developing minds and talents.

As a coach, our role is to help our mentees acquire new skills. It is important to motivate them to learn and teach them how to do so effectively. Good coaching bridges the gap between theory and practice. A successful coach is sincerely involved in listening, questioning, and being responsive. We should encourage our mentees to experiment with new behaviors. Additionally, it is essential to recognize that each individual is unique and possesses different potential. Great coaches consistently push their mentees to excel in all their endeavors.

Satya Nadella's Mentoring of Microsoft Employees

When Satya Nadella became CEO of Microsoft in 2014, he observed that the company was struggling with internal competition, complacency, and a rigid culture. He began interacting with managers and employees at various levels of the organization. After numerous rounds of discussion, he found that his managers lacked a leadership approach and that employees were hesitant to take risks because their managers were rigid and did not provide any freedom to fail.

Nadella decided to launch a company-wide mentoring program aimed at transforming his managers into exceptional leaders. The goal is to build a culture where new ideas are welcomed, employees have the freedom to fail, and are encouraged to take risks. All employees will be tutored to develop a growth mindset and a continuous learning attitude.

With the help of newly developed leadership skills among managers at various levels of Microsoft, Nadella shifted the company culture from a know-it-all to a learn-it-all attitude. Through consistent mentoring at all levels, employees became more engaged with innovation. They adopted a growth mindset, leading Microsoft to emerge as a leader in cloud computing and AI.

6.2 Counseling

Many employees within the organization struggle with specific emotional issues. To address these issues, leaders must fulfill their role as counselors. Although counselors are highly trained therapists, this is not a job for untrained individuals. However, great leaders develop some counseling skills to assist their subordinates and refer certain cases to professional therapists when necessary. Counseling is a therapeutic approach in which the counselor listens to clients and helps them identify and manage emotional issues. Mentors utilize counseling skills to support learners who are struggling. Counseling is a process of helping clients find effective ways to address their problems rather than simply providing advice or telling them what to do. Figure 6.4 illustrates four key steps that a leader can take to counsel their subordinates.

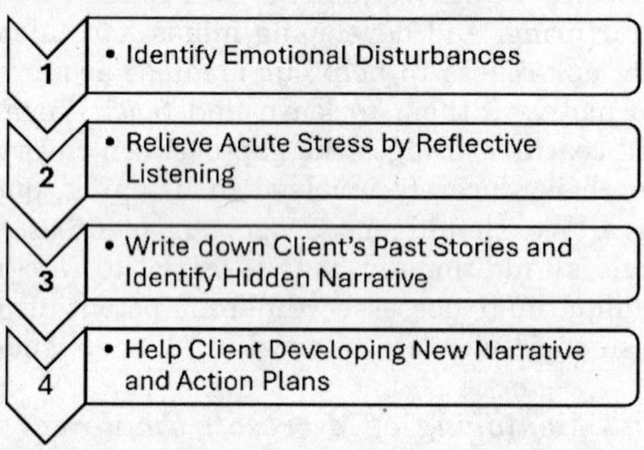

FIGURE 6.4 Steps in Counseling.

6.2.1 Steps in Counseling

1. *Identify Mentees with Emotional Disturbances*

In their role as counselors, leaders observe their followers' behavior in extreme situations. People often react to challenges by changing their behavior significantly; for instance, a shy person may become even more withdrawn or, conversely, become overly verbal. Additionally, individuals who are emotionally disturbed may exhibit behaviors such as excessive laughing or overeating.

Some employees occasionally experience high levels of anxiety, which can manifest through panic behavior, tense facial expressions, or heavy perspiration. In rare instances, some individuals may have complete breakdowns, causing them to lose control over their thoughts,

feelings, or actions, leading to irrational thinking. Cases of severe breakdowns should be referred to a professional psychotherapist.

2. *Relieve Acute Stress by Reflective Listening*

Counselors take the time to sit with their clients and listen patiently to them. Through reflective listening, they encourage clients to share their past difficulties or current challenges. This exploration can uncover various issues, such as mental stress, past traumas, and resistance to change.

Listening plays a crucial role in counseling. It allows counselors to explore the root causes of their mentees' emotional disturbances while also helping to alleviate feelings of frustration, anxiety, and fear. Reflective listening, which involves asking questions, is an essential skill of counselors. They are trained to ask exploratory and open-ended questions that clarify various issues, uncover hidden emotions, and validate their clients' feelings, words, and past experiences.

3. *Write down the Client's Past Stories and Experiences, and Identify Hidden Narratives*

In addition to reflective listening, writing down the client's past stories and experiences can help the counselor identify any traumatic events stored in the client's emotional memory. If such experiences exist, this approach can reveal the hidden narratives in the client's subconscious mind.

For instance, if a client experiences rejection in childhood and this traumatic event becomes ingrained in their emotional psyche, they may develop underlying beliefs such as "I will be rejected" or "I am destined to be rejected." As a result of these beliefs, the client might feel compelled to protect themselves from further rejection. This could lead them to avoid taking the initiative or to feel shy about forming friendships. Consequently, they may struggle to be an effective team player.

4. *Help the Client Develop New Narratives and Action Plans*

The counselor should assist the client in developing and writing new narratives and action plans to facilitate their experience.

In relation to the example above, one can create new narratives, such as "I am well-accepted by others" or "People love and admire my skills." When these new narratives are deeply embedded in the client's subconscious mind, they can foster the emergence of new needs, like the need for love and affection.

Consistent actions are necessary to meet new needs. These actions may include efforts to gain knowledge, develop new skills, and embrace positive traits such as sincerity and discipline. The more we satisfy the new need for love and affection, the more we can replace any previously problematic narratives with a more positive outlook.

Ed Catmull and the Hidden Fear at Pixar

Ed Catmull, the co-founder of Pixar, once noted that employees, especially the junior ones, do not feel safe sharing their honest opinions when they disagree with senior management. On the surface, everything appeared to be fine. However, Ed sensed that junior employees were not expressing their true thoughts. He decided to explore the hidden narratives in their minds. Through private conversations, he discovered the following hidden narratives.

- They believed that speaking up against their seniors could hurt their careers.
- They believed that only seniors had the right to challenge creative ideas or the status quo.
- They feared failure, which could damage their reputation.

After identifying these hidden narratives, Ed implemented measures to build new narratives in the minds of junior employees.

- Ed provided psychological security to junior employees by reassuring them that at Pixer, we value open debate. Failure is an inherent part of the creative process and will ultimately be rewarded.
- He established a platform where directors, animators, and writers could critique ideas without a hierarchical structure, allowing junior employees to challenge their seniors.
- By openly acknowledging his mistakes, Ed encouraged his senior employees to break the fear-driven mindset of junior employees.

By addressing hidden narratives and creating new ones, Ed tackled the issue of fear at Pixar and strengthened the creative culture. As a result, junior employees became more confident in voicing their ideas, challenging the status quo, and critiquing the ideas of senior staff, which led to continuous innovation. This approach enabled Pixar to produce milestone films such as *Inside Out* and *Coco*.

ASSESSMENTS

1. What is mentoring? Explain the different steps involved in the mentoring process.
2. What is counseling? Explain the different steps involved in the counseling process.

CHAPTER 7

Motivation

7.1 Motivation

Motivation comes from the word "motive," which refers to an individual's drives, needs, or desires. When a person shows willingness and puts in effort to achieve specific goals to satisfy their needs or desires, that is Motivation. It is a crucial link between knowing and doing, thinking and action, and competence and performance.

Industrial psychologists have extensively researched and proposed various need-based and behavioral motivational theories. The primary distinction between need-based and behavioral motivational theories lies in their approaches to defining what drives human motivation to exert effort. Need-based motivational theories focus on how the interaction between a human's internal needs and external influences generates motivation. They suggest that humans act in specific ways to fulfill their biological and psychological needs. Need-based theories try to explain why people are motivated.

In contrast, behavioral motivation theories focus on external factors and reinforcements that drive motivation to behave in a certain way. They stress that rewards, punishments, and learned behaviors influence motivation. Behavioral motivation theories try to explain how external factors and human cognition interact to influence motivation.

A leader's primary role is to inspire employees to willingly put their efforts into achieving both organizational and personal goals. Inspiring employees involves a series of processes that guide behavioral choices. Before exploring how leaders motivate their teams, it is essential to understand various motivational theories based on human needs and behavior.

7.2 Need-Based Motivational Theories

Human needs can broadly be divided into biological and psychological categories. These needs help humans survive and thrive in the world. While thousands of words in the English language describe different types of needs, it can be overwhelming to define them all. Therefore, behavior scientists have grouped several needs into specific categories using regression models, developing various need-based motivational models. Some of the most widely used need-based motivational theories are discussed below:

7.2.1 Maslow's Hierarchy of Needs

Abraham Maslow proposed a hierarchy of five categories of human needs, as illustrated in Figure 7.1. He organized these categories in order of priority, ranging from the most basic needs (Physiological) to the most complex needs (Self-Actualization). According to Maslow, when a person's needs at one level are largely satisfied, the next level of needs becomes the primary focus. To effectively motivate someone, it's essential to understand the level of the need hierarchy they are currently at and concentrate on fulfilling their needs at that level or higher.

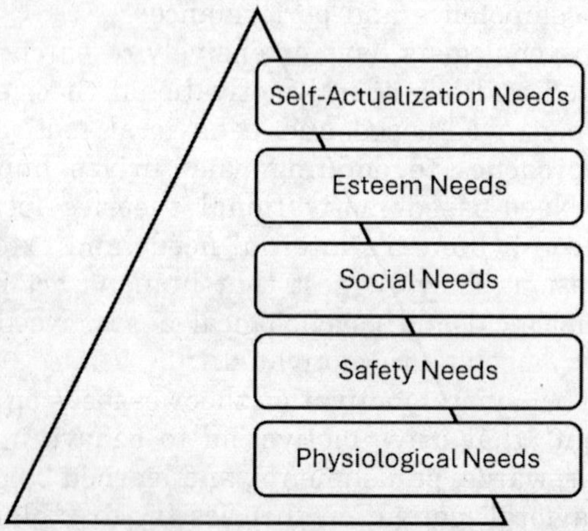

FIGURE 7.1 Maslow's Hierarchy of Needs.

An individual moves to the next level of need once the current level has been minimally satisfied. Leaders apply this theory to improve job design, plan compensation and rewards, develop training programs, and create organizational policies and practices that address employees' needs. The five categories of needs are discussed below:

1. *Physiological Needs*

People have basic bodily needs like food, water, sex, and clothing. To address these needs, leaders often provide adequate salaries, promote employees to higher-paying positions, and offer financial incentives and rewards. They may also implement gift schemes, various types of allowances, and other benefits.

2. *Safety Needs*

The need for shelter, job security, life stability, and health safety are significant in this category. To address these needs, the leader provides job security, retirement benefits, and pension plans, and ensures a clean and hygienic workplace. Additionally, they offer life and health insurance and emergency medical facilities on the workplace premises.

3. *Social Needs*

Social needs encompass the need for affiliation, friendship, love, affection, social acceptance, and a sense of belonging. To meet these needs, leaders create opportunities for meaningful social interactions by organizing conferences, workshops, presentations, annual meetings, and regular celebrations to recognize successful goal accomplishments. Nowadays, many companies sponsor their productive employees to gain memberships in social clubs, country clubs, and sports clubs.

4. *Esteem Needs*

Esteem needs include the desire for respect, social status, recognition, and enhanced self-esteem. Leaders recognize these needs by awarding achievement certificates during the organization's annual meetings, publishing success stories in the company newsletter, writing appreciation letters to high achievers, and encouraging others to applaud those who reach their goals during celebration events.

5. *Self-Actualization Needs*

People under this need category want to become the best expression of themselves. They want to utilize their potential fully. Their self-actualization needs are satisfied when they generate extraordinary performance, learn new skills, develop competencies, and acquire excellent knowledge. They want to be highly creative and express themselves in a significant manner. To satisfy their self-actualization needs, leaders help them chart their careers, provide opportunities to learn new skills and develop competencies in their passionate area, and send them abroad for training and education.

7.2.2 Alderfer's ERG Theory of Motivation

Clayton Alderfer modified Maslow's five needs categories into three, as shown in Figure 7.2. Unlike Maslow's theory, Alderfer argued that individuals can pursue multiple needs simultaneously and may regress

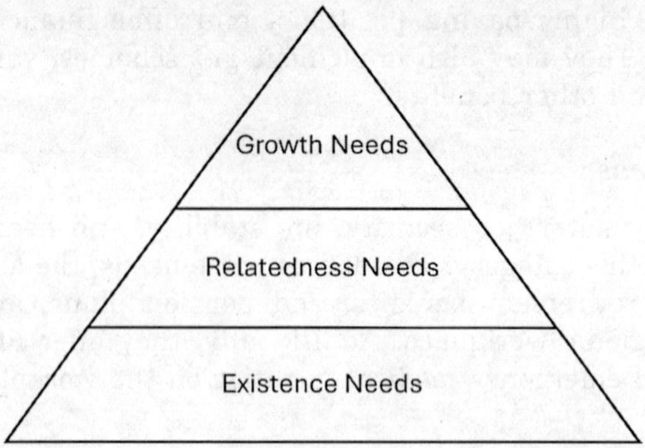

FIGURE 7.2 Alderfer's ERG Theory of Motivation.

to lower-order needs if their current needs are not satisfied. Alderfer referred to this phenomenon as the Frustration-Regression Principle. The three need categories are defined as follows:

1. *Existence (E) Needs*

Existence needs are humans' most basic survival requirements, encompassing their physical well-being, security, and financial stability. Existence needs include food, water, shelter, clothing, sleep, health, financial security, job stability, and protection from harm. When designing salary packages and job benefits, organizations ensure that employees' basic needs are met.

2. *Relatedness (R) Needs*

Every human wants to feel connected to their community and society. They strive to be valued, accepted, and loved by others. People want to develop meaningful interpersonal relationships and embrace a sense of belonging. Leaders implement various strategies to meet the relatedness needs of their employees. Some essential strategies include the following:

- Creating an organizational climate where employees feel valued and respected.
- Organize informal gatherings, outings, and networking events.
- Develop and implement diversity and inclusion programs.
- Promote a transparent culture where employees can freely express their feelings.
- Celebrate small wins, achievements, birthdays, and work anniversaries.
- Establish a peer recognition program to foster appreciation for employees among colleagues.

3. *Growth Needs*

Growth needs are individuals' desires for personal development, accomplishments, and career advancement. Personal development encompasses intellectual growth, emotional maturity, and the development of skills and competencies. Meaningful accomplishments involve completing tasks that are exceptionally valuable to the organization and contribute positively to people's lives. Career advancement primarily concerns obtaining promotions within the organization and reaching top positions. To meet the growth needs of employees, leaders do the following:

- Leaders and employees mutually set organizational and personal goals.
- Leaders mentor employees to facilitate their growth, ensuring continuous learning through targeted courses and training.
- Leaders assign challenging tasks and higher responsibilities to their employees, offering them autonomy in decision-making.
- Leaders promote work-life balance among employees, enabling them to pursue hobbies and cultivate creative and innovative skills.

7.2.3 McClelland's Theory of Needs

David McClelland argued that three key categories of needs drive individuals the most. These three categories are illustrated in Figure 7.3 below.

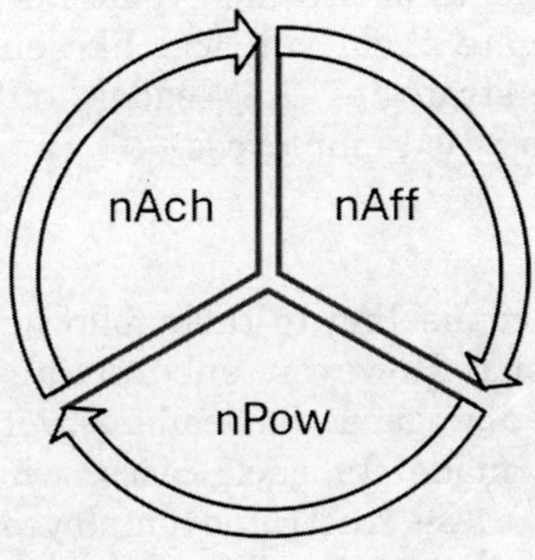

FIGURE 7.3 McClelland's Theory of Needs.

1. **Need for Achievement (nAch):** The need for achievement, symbolized by 'nAch,' drives individuals to pursue challenging goals, accomplish exceptional feats, and strive for excellence in all their endeavors. To fulfill employees' need for achievement, leaders should establish challenging yet attainable goals, provide them with autonomy to make decisions, and assign tasks that

align with their strengths. Leaders foster a competitive yet supportive environment, promoting teamwork while ensuring that individual contributions are recognized and encouraging creative and innovative problem-solving approaches.

2. **Need for Affiliation (nAff):** An individual's desire to build warm, friendly, and harmonious relationships with others is known as the need for affiliation. People with a strong need for affiliation seek approval, a sense of belonging, and validation from those around them. They tend to prefer working in teams over working independently. To fulfill this need, leaders can create team-based roles, celebrate small achievements, and encourage informal gatherings within the organization.
3. **Need for Power (nPow):** The need for power refers to an individual's desire to lead others, exert control over situations, and attain social status. People with a strong need for power often become charismatic and persuasive leaders capable of driving organizational change effectively. To satisfy employees with a high need for power, leaders can offer them leadership roles, empower them to expand their influence, and publicly acknowledge their contributions and successes.

7.2.4 Herzberg's Two-Factor Motivation Theory

Frederick Herzberg suggested that merely meeting employees' basic needs will not sustain their motivation within an organization. He argued that when employees are disinterested or frustrated due to a poor organizational climate or strained relationships with supervisors, any attempts to motivate them will feel like empty gestures. Let us explore the ineffective strategies that leaders often use in an attempt to motivate their dissatisfied employees.

1. *Positive Kick*

Leaders offer positive counseling to their followers by highlighting the benefits of their actions. However, subordinates who are frustrated with the system may disregard the leader's words, believing that no improvements will be made. In such cases, when we try to provide positive counseling to these frustrated employees, they may perceive it as a positive kick in the pants. This scenario raises the question of who is truly motivated: the leader or the employees? Of course, it is a leader who is motivated.

2. *Negative Kick*

When we struggle to persuade our team through positive counseling, we often resort to a different method: negative counseling, where we emphasize the negative consequences of their actions. However, this approach yields the same result among our followers. They perceive our words as a negative kick in the pants. They will hear us with one ear but ignore everything we say with the other. This scenario, again, raises the question of who is truly motivated. The leader or the followers. Definitely, it is a leader who is motivated and not the followers.

3. *Real Kick*

When nothing seems to work, we feel that the time has come to implement things the hard way. We impose certain consequences, such as explanation calls, salary deductions, and suspensions, to get our employees back on track. People view these punishments as a real kick in the pants. Once again, who is motivated— the leader or the followers?

4. *Return Kick*

In response to a real kick, followers retaliate with a return kick, such as resignation, a court case, violence, etc.

In light of the above scenario, Herzberg emphasized the need to develop a motivational ecosystem within the organization. To achieve this, he classified motivation into two categories: Hygiene Factors and Growth Factors. Examples of both types of factors are illustrated in Figure 7.4.

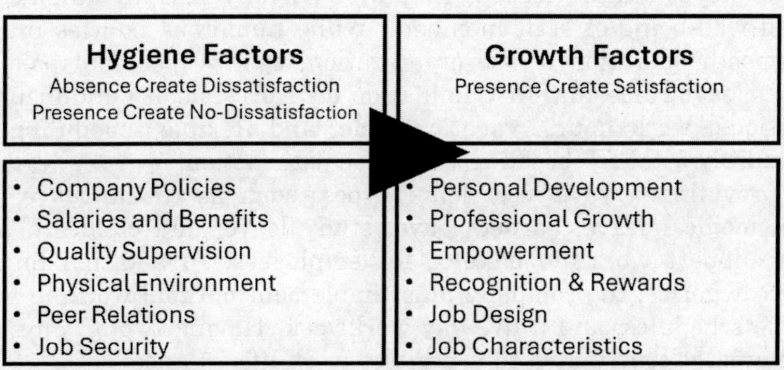

FIGURE 7.4 Herzberg's Two-Factor Motivation Theory.

Herzberg further articulated that the absence of hygiene factors leads to dissatisfaction. However, simply having hygiene factors present, without growth factors, results in a state of neutrality, where employees are neither satisfied nor dissatisfied. We must focus on growth factors to help employees transition from dissatisfaction to satisfaction.

To achieve the desired results from growth factors, it is essential first to ensure that hygiene factors are present in the organizational climate and that employees are free from dissatisfaction. As illustrated in Figure 7.4, leaders can establish hygiene factors such as employee-friendly policies, quality supervision, adequate salaries, a pleasant physical environment, productive peer relationships, and job security. By addressing these factors, leaders can meet employees' physiological, security, and social needs. Once these needs are met, employees will attain a state of no dissatisfaction.

Leaders can address higher-order needs, including esteem and self-actualization, by establishing growth factors such as personal development, professional growth, empowerment, recognition, rewards, and engaging job characteristics. This approach helps generate intrinsic motivation and fosters a state of flow among employees. For instance, personal development and professional growth directly fulfill individuals' needs for self-actualization, enabling them to become the best expression of themselves. Additionally, performance recognition and rewards help meet employees' esteem needs, while empowerment and improved job characteristics contribute to intrinsic motivation and a more engaging work experience.

A. Hygiene Factors

1. *Company's Policies*

Company policies are established guidelines aimed at assisting employers in managing administrative, health, safety, regulatory, legal, customer, and employee-related issues. Employee-friendly policies enhance the overall well-being of staff members. While numerous policies promote the smooth operation of the organization, specific personal policies—such as leave rules, anti-discrimination measures, health and insurance provisions, work hours, vacation time, and flexible scheduling—are particularly vital for boosting employee satisfaction.

Providing a variety of leave types, such as casual leave, duty leave, medical leave, earned leave, study leave, and childcare leave, helps support work-life balance for employees. In addition to these leave categories, the company must implement optimal working hours, flexible schedules, and a five-day workweek. Having two off days each week greatly contributes to a positive work-life balance.

To enhance employee morale and cultivate a sense of belonging, the company should implement a strict policy against discrimination and guarantee equal opportunities for all employees.

It is essential to protect employees' health and family interests by providing health and life insurance policies for each employee. The policy for maintaining health hygiene in the workplace must be diligently implemented.

2. *Salary and Benefits*

Salary is a fixed compensation paid at regular intervals (monthly or annually) to employees for their work in the form of money. Wages are paid hourly. What salary can protect workers from dissatisfaction?

While there is no set limit to the salary paid to employees based on their qualifications and job profile, it should align with industry standards at each level.

Furthermore, a good salary should cover the basic needs and lifestyles of employees and their families, allowing them to save money for unforeseen events and future security. Salaries should be supplemented with various benefits, including health and life insurance, vacation pay, maternity leave, employer contributions to retirement plans such as provident funds and pensions, stock options, and bonuses.

3. *Quality Supervision*

Quality supervision entails supporting and motivating employees to excel in their tasks and attain remarkable results. Recent research findings and supervisory practices show that effective supervisors have the essential managerial, leadership, and communication skills required to provide support and guidance to their employees in the workplace.

Supervisors should avoid micromanaging their subordinates; instead, they should offer autonomy, empowerment, and emotional support. Effective supervisors cultivate productive relationships with their colleagues, build strong teams, manage change effectively, oversee workflow, provide on-the-job training, evaluate performance, offer constructive feedback, resolve employees' issues and disputes, and provide mentoring support to their subordinates.

4. *Relationship with Peers*

Strong peer-to-peer relationships in the workplace greatly enhance employee engagement and motivation. They reduce turnover and protect against job dissatisfaction. Key elements of robust peer relationships include mutual trust and respect, teamwork, a win-win attitude, and effective communication among employees. These connections can also serve as valuable references and networks for employees in their future careers.

5. *Physical Environment*

A positive physical environment in the workplace enhances employee productivity. It elevates both the psychological and physical energy of individuals, boosting their morale and spirits. Proper lighting, a quiet atmosphere, a comfortable room temperature, clean air with a pleasant scent, dust-free furniture, and well-maintained office floors and restrooms all contribute to improved concentration and productivity among workers.

6. *Job Security*

All the hygiene factors mentioned above may not yield the desired results unless there is a strong sense of job security within the organization. Every employee seeks job security and stability in their lives. When employees feel insecure, it becomes challenging for them to perform at their best. Many employees are currently concerned that they may be replaced by new graduates who are willing to work for lower wages. Additionally, large-scale automation in companies, where machines and robots are increasingly taking over human roles, adds to the fear of being laid off.

Managers should communicate to employees that they are valued, safe, secure, and have a promising future within the organization. However, simply communicating positive messages is not enough; effective mentoring is crucial for developing employees into skilled, competent, knowledgeable, diligent, and valuable team members. Job insecurity and the perception of adding value cannot coexist in the workplace. When an employee demonstrates outstanding performance and contributes significantly to the organization, their job insecurity will naturally diminish.

B. Growth Factors

1. *Personal Development*

Personal growth is evaluated by how effectively individuals reach their life goals, recognize their potential, and embrace wisdom and values. Organizations frequently implement development programs to cultivate their employees' potential, character, and values. Ultimately, personal growth results in enhanced maturity, success, and life satisfaction.

Managers, in their role as mentors, play a crucial part in motivating their mentees to invest in their personal development consistently. Mentors help employees understand the significance of ongoing self-improvement in achieving their life goals and overall satisfaction. Companies often organize various employee development programs that focus on key areas, including personality development, communication skills, emotional intelligence, leadership skills, sales skills, and life management skills.

2. *Professional Growth*

Professional growth for employees entails acquiring new skills and work experience, achieving job objectives, delivering exceptional performance, and progressing to higher positions within the organizational hierarchy. To facilitate their employees' professional growth, many companies employ various strategies, such as promoting from within, aligning organizational goals with individual needs, forming cross-functional teams, and offering learning resources.

Promoting from within is one of the most effective ways to motivate employees to remain with a company, invest in their skill development, and deliver outstanding performance. A Gallup study found that nearly one-third of employees leave their jobs due to a lack of career advancement or promotional opportunities within the organization. Internal promotions boost employee engagement and encourage professional development. Additionally, cross-functional teams enable employees to acquire new skills and assume roles that extend beyond their job descriptions.

3. *Empowerment*

Many leaders and organizations assign job responsibilities to workers without granting them any autonomy or authority. In this situation, workers often feel micromanaged and powerless, which can lead to frustration and demotivation. Workers must seek approval from their leaders for any decision, which slows down the process and reduces both individual productivity and overall organizational efficiency. This constant demand for approvals places a significant burden on leaders, creating bottlenecks that hinder effective workflows and generate conflicts between workers and their leaders. Workers often find their jobs unfulfilling due to a lack of authority and autonomy, which can lead to a loss of responsibility for the outcomes of their work.

Leaders should empower their employees by granting them apparent authority and the autonomy to make their own decisions. In other words, leaders should give their workers the freedom to fail because making decisions carries the risk of making mistakes. However, this should not lead to the revocation of authority and autonomy from employees.

4. *Recognition and Rewards*

To appreciate and motivate employees, the company recognizes and rewards exceptional performance. Appreciation is a fundamental human need that should never be overlooked, as employees desire acknowledgment for their contributions. When their work is recognized and rewarded, job satisfaction increases significantly. Rewards can be classified into two main forms: cash and non-cash. Cash rewards are given to high-performing employees in the form of salary increases, bonuses, or incentives. Non-cash rewards are also highly effective and can take various forms, which are detailed below:

- **Handwritten Notes:** The top executive, like the CEO or director, pens a personal handwritten note of appreciation to employees for their outstanding performance.
- **Executive Offer a Cup of Coffee:** Top executives invite high-performing employees to their offices for a cup of coffee and discuss the company and its business with them.
- **Free Leave Pass:** The company offers employees a specified number of free days off for personal use. They can travel to

exotic locations, read books, play with their kids, and enjoy other recreational activities.

- **Love from Co-workers:** Co-workers write something they sincerely admire about an employee on a vibrant sheet of paper and then frame that paper alongside a photograph of the employee.
- **Applaud with Standing Ovation:** High-performing employees receive a standing ovation from all the employees at the annual general meeting.
- **Wall of Fame:** Employees who achieve something extraordinary are selected to have their photos displayed, along with details of their accomplishments, on a Wall of Fame located within the company's premises.

5. *Job Design*

A job consists of a series of tasks and activities that engage an individual within an organization. Job design is a deliberate process of organizing tasks, responsibilities, and authority into a cohesive unit of work to achieve specific goals. A well-designed job can enhance employees' intrinsic motivation and promote a state of flow, leading to exceptional performance. In contrast, poorly designed jobs can result in monotony, job dissatisfaction, high employee turnover, and decreased performance. There are two primary methods for redesigning jobs: job enlargement and job enrichment.

- **Job Enlargement:** Job enlargement refers to the horizontal expansion of job activities. It involves adding various tasks that are at the same level within the organization, thereby broadening the scope of an existing job. This approach helps employees overcome monotony by allowing them to engage in a wider range of tasks. Additionally, it enables employees to acquire diverse skills, which can lead to higher wages and better career advancement opportunities. For instance, a teacher, instead of merely teaching a course in class, may feel more motivated when given a chance to develop course content, deliver lectures, assess students, and submit final grades to the board of studies.
- **Job Enrichment:** Job enrichment involves the vertical expansion of job activities. It is a vertical loading of motivating activities on the existing job. The existing job can be enriched by adding a few more activities from the upper level to make the existing job more challenging, creative, exciting, and rewarding. Additionally, job enrichment provides jobholders with greater autonomy and decision-making power. For example, the Ritz-Carlton Hotel permits every employee to spend up to $2,000 to satisfy any single guest without seeking permission from the general manager.

6. *Job Characteristics Model*

Many organizations are now utilizing the Job Characteristics Model to design a variety of jobs that effectively motivate employees. Figure 7.5 illustrates various job characteristics, along with the psychological states and outcomes associated with them.

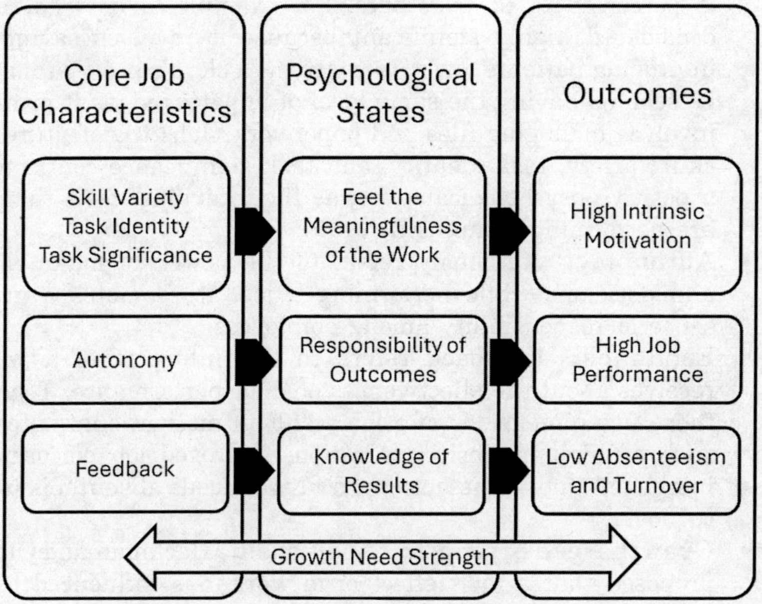

FIGURE 7.5 Job Characteristics Model.

The Job Characteristics Model, developed by Hackman and Oldham, outlines various job attributes to consider when designing roles involving diverse tasks. This model is primarily divided into three broad categories: core job characteristics, psychological states, and outcomes. The core characteristics of a job include skill variety, task identity, task significance, autonomy, and feedback.

- **Skill Variety:** Skill variety refers to the range of skills that a worker uses to complete their tasks. Greater skill variety can significantly reduce job monotony. For example, an assembly line worker typically employs only a few skills and performs repetitive tasks, while an engineer designing a machine uses a wider array of skills.
- **Task Identity:** Task identity refers to the completeness of a job, indicating the degree to which a worker engages in an entire task from start to finish. For instance, in an automobile company, an assembly line worker has a low task identity because they only carry out a small portion of the overall process of car production. In contrast, a college teacher has a

high level of task identity because they are responsible for the complete process of teaching a course. This includes designing the course, preparing handouts and exam papers, delivering lectures, and assigning grades to students.

- **Task Significance:** The significance of a task refers to the impact a job has on others and how meaningful that job is perceived to be by others. For example, a doctor's role is considered highly significant because it involves saving and improving patients' lives. In contrast, a clerk's position may not be seen as having the same level of importance, as it primarily involves managing files and paperwork. Jobs that feature high skill variety, task identity, and task significance contribute to a positive psychological state, as the individual feels that they are performing meaningful work.
- **Autonomy:** Autonomy refers to the power to make choices and decisions while performing a job. It promotes a greater sense of responsibility among employees.
- **Feedback:** Feedback refers to the information a worker receives about the effectiveness of their performance. Together, these five dimensions of a job result in motivational outcomes, such as high intrinsic motivation, improved job performance, increased job satisfaction, and reduced absenteeism and turnover.
- **Growth Need Strength:** Additionally, Hackman and Oldham proposed that a job's effect on a worker is influenced by the strength of their growth needs. Thus, the existence of **strong growth needs** in people will lead to more significant outcomes.

7.3 Behavioral Motivational Theories

As narrated earlier, behavioral motivation theories aim to explain how external factors (such as rewards, punishments, reinforcements, and social influence) and internal factors (such as self-esteem and self-efficacy) shape individuals' motivation and influence their behavior. The following are some important behavioral theories of motivation.

7.3.1 Goal Setting Theory

Edwin Locke suggested that having intentions to pursue a goal is a significant source of motivation in the workplace. According to goal-setting theory, an individual's behavior is influenced by the goals they establish for themselves. Performance improves with specific and challenging goals.

People adjust their level of effort in response to the challenges presented by their goals. Goals provide direction for employees, and achieving these goals is rewarding as it fulfills their esteem needs and motivates them to pursue higher goals in the future. Challenging yet attainable goals help regulate individuals' efforts, enhance their persistence, and encourage them to develop effective strategies for completing tasks.

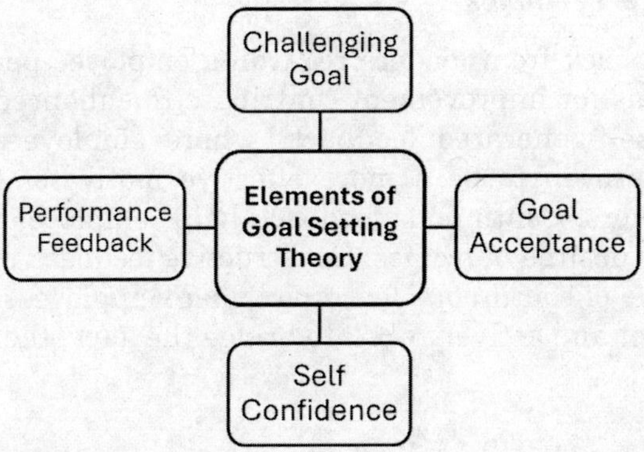

FIGURE 7.6 Elements of Goal Setting Theory.

Figure 7.6 illustrates four key elements that should be incorporated into the goal-setting model to ensure effective performance.

1. *Challenging and Specific Goals*

Goals must be clear, specific, challenging, and achievable. Challenging goals motivate individuals to put in rigorous effort and remain engaged. It encourages individuals to think outside the box and develop innovative strategies to achieve their goals. Challenging goals eliminate any possibility of procrastination. Specific goals provide a clear direction, allowing individuals to adopt a more focused approach toward achieving them.

2. *Goal Acceptance and Commitment*

People need to accept the goal and commit to it emotionally. To generate acceptance and commitment, employees must develop goals in consultation with their leaders. Accepting goals enhances intrinsic motivation and persistence, even in the face of obstacles. Imposed and unaccepted goals generate stress and resistance among employees, whereas accepted goals cultivate a sense of ownership and enhance performance.

3. *Self-confidence to achieve the goal*

Self-efficacy refers to an individual's belief in possessing the necessary skills, competency, and capability to accomplish a task. High self-efficacy indicates greater confidence in one's ability to succeed. Research shows that individuals with low self-efficacy beliefs may reduce their efforts or discontinue their attempts altogether. Self-confidence influences our mindset, boosts motivation, reduces fear of failure, strengthens resilience, and increases our persistence.

4. *Performance Feedback*

Consistent feedback from leaders regarding employee performance and identifying areas for improvement contribute to enhanced performance. Additionally, self-generated feedback, where employees assess their progress, has proven to be a more effective motivator than feedback provided by others. Continuous feedback helps employees to align their efforts with the desired outcomes. Constructive feedback on performance fosters a culture of continuous learning, where employees identify areas for improvement and actively work to bridge the gaps, thereby achieving their goals.

7.3.2 Equity Theory of Motivation

J.S. Adams developed the equity theory of motivation, which suggests that employees have strong expectations for justice and fairness within their organizations. This theory identifies two key variables: inputs and outcomes. The inputs encompass the time, effort, education, experience, training, ideas, and abilities that employees invest in their work to complete tasks.

In the context of equity theory, outcomes are distinct from task accomplishments. Instead, outcomes refer to the rewards that individuals receive from the organization for their work. Examples of outcomes include pay, promotions, recognition, job security, personal development, and benefits. Individuals compare their job inputs and outcomes with those of others. If they perceive any inequity, they react strongly to eliminate it. This comparison can be somewhat subjective, as it relies on personal perceptions and feelings.

Figure 7.7 illustrates the equation of equity theory, which suggests that a person's input-outcome ratio must be perceived as equivalent to the input-outcome ratios of others.

X Outcome / Input	=	Y Outcome / Input

FIGURE 7.7 Equation of Equity Theory.

When an individual feels that his input-outcome ratio is roughly on par with others at the same level, he feels satisfied. The problem arises when these ratios are unbalanced. In either case of positive or negative imbalance, people experience some tension or anxiety and seek to reduce the perceived inequity.

Positive inequity occurs when an individual receives a higher reward than others for the same inputs. Negative inequity occurs when an individual receives a lower reward than others for the same inputs. People adjust their efforts to alleviate their anxiety. In response to inequity, the following behavioral changes commonly occur in organizations:

1. **Changing inputs:** A person can increase or decrease their efforts in the organization, for instance, by working harder or, conversely, by working less hard.
2. **Changing outcomes:** A person may try to improve their outcomes by expressing disagreement and requesting better rewards from upper management.
3. **Changing perception of self:** Instead of changing the inputs or outcomes, people might alter their perceptions. For example, if they feel overpaid, they might think, "I am better than others." Conversely, if they feel underpaid, they might believe, "I'm not as competent," or think another person has a better relationship with the supervisor.
4. **Choose a different referent:** A person may feel uncomfortable comparing himself to a better performer. In this case, he may choose someone else for comparison, whom he perceives as inferior.
5. **Leave the field:** If people perceive that they cannot obtain justice, they may request a transfer to another unit or location. In extreme cases, they may even leave the organization.

How to Utilize the Equity Theory of Motivation

By applying the Equity Theory of Motivation, leaders can effectively enhance job satisfaction and productivity while reducing employee turnover. Proper implementation of equity theory requires the following actions.

- Maintain a system of equitable compensation and rewards aligned with employees' contributions.
- Cultivate a culture of transparent communication that includes clear explanations about compensation structures, promotion policies, performance evaluation criteria, and management decisions.
- Create an employee feedback system that allows employees to express concerns about fairness, enabling management to implement appropriate measures to ensure equity.
- Organizations should implement a system of performance-based incentives to adequately recognize employees' contributions.
- Distribute the tasks fairly and ensure that employees do not feel overburdened compared to others.

- Conduct employee surveys or individual meetings to assess employees' perceptions of equity.

7.3.3 Expectancy Theory of Motivation

Victor Vroom developed the Expectancy Theory of Motivation, proposing that before individuals exert effort to complete a task, they hold specific expectations regarding the connection between their efforts and the resulting performance level. Additionally, they believe that this performance will lead to rewards that will be aligned with their personal preferences.

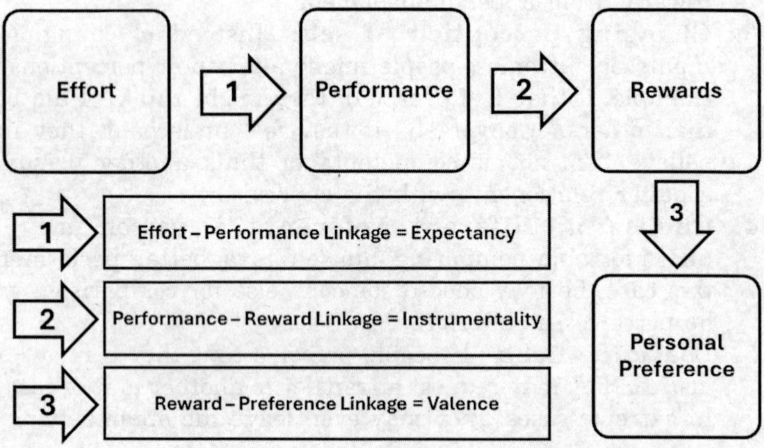

FIGURE 7.8 Expectancy Theory of Motivation.

Figure 7.8 illustrates Vroom's Expectancy Theory of Motivation, showing three linkages leading to three variables: Expectancy, Instrumentality, and Valence. These variables, individually and in combination, generate varying motivation levels among individuals to work.

Effort – Performance Linkage = Expectancy

Expectancy refers to how much a person believes their efforts will successfully lead to completing a task. They may question whether their efforts will meet the performance expectations set by management. This concept represents the connection between effort and performance, ranging from 0 to 1. Suppose an individual perceives that the chances of achieving a positive outcome are zero. In that case, they are unlikely to attempt the task. Conversely, if their expectancy is high, they are more likely to invest greater effort to achieve the desired results.

Performance – Reward Linkage = Instrumentality

Instrumentality refers to the likelihood of a specific performance leading to a desired reward. For example, suppose individuals are informed that performing exceptionally well will result in a promotion. In that case, they must believe their outstanding performance is crucial for attaining that promotion. Furthermore, it is vital that the supervisor who promises the reward possesses the actual authority to grant it. The value of instrumentality ranges from 0 to 1, indicating the perceived probability of receiving the reward.

Reward – Personal preference Linkage = Valence

Valence refers to the strength of an individual's preference for receiving a reward, reflecting the value they place on it. This value is subjective and varies from person to person. For instance, a promotion may hold high valence for younger employees. In contrast, senior employees may place greater value on responsibility, authority, and respect. Valence can be positive or negative, depending on an individual's preferences for a specific reward. If a person feels indifferent toward a reward, their valence is considered zero. Therefore, the total range of valence spans from –1 to +1.

According to Vroom, motivation is a result of expectancy, instrumentality, and valence. Vroom provides the following formula to calculate the levels of motivation among individuals:

$$\text{Motivation} = \text{Expectancy} \times \text{Instrumentality} \times \text{Valence}$$

The expectancy model comprises three factors that can combine in numerous ways, depending on the levels of valence, expectancy, and instrumentality. The combination that generates the strongest motivation is when all three factors are high: high expectancy, high instrumentality, and high positive valence. Conversely, if all three factors are low, motivation will be weak. Since the model operates on a multiplicative basis, if any one of the factors approaches zero, the likelihood of motivated performance also approaches zero.

Managerial Implications of Expectancy Theory

(a) To maximize expectancy, help the person feel competent in achieving the desired performance level. This should be achieved in the following way:
- Identify and develop employees' potential through nurturing leadership.
- Provide effective training and support for work efforts.
- Clarify the performance objectives.
- Assist them in breaking the task into manageable subtasks.

(b) To maximize instrumentality, help our employees feel confident about the rewards by following these steps:
- Clarify and remove doubts from people's minds.
- Build trust and be credible.

- Make the appraisal technique and reward policy more transparent and contingent.

(c) To maximize valence, help the individual understand the value of all potential rewards and guide them on what to expect. Set employees' expectation levels through a proper mentoring process. Identify each person's needs and adjust the rewards to align with those needs.

7.3.4 Self-Determination Theory of Motivation

Self-determination theory was developed by professors Richard Ryan and Edward Deci at the University of Rochester to explain the conditions that foster intrinsic motivation. Within this theory, intrinsic motivation is defined as our inclination toward spontaneous interest, exploration, and the pursuit of mastery over new information, skills, and experiences.

Intrinsic motivation occurs when we engage in activities purely for the enjoyment they bring. For example, we might sing a song alone simply because we enjoy singing. This type of motivation arises during the activity itself and offers its rewards. Research has shown that intrinsically motivated individuals often display greater confidence, interest, involvement, and excitement in their tasks. They exhibit higher persistence, self-esteem, and subjective well-being when intrinsically motivated. Subjective well-being refers to a state filled with positive emotions.

Extrinsic motivation encourages us to perform tasks because they lead to desirable outcomes or help us avoid harmful situations. For instance, we often work to earn money to cover essential needs like food and housing, or put in extra effort to complete tasks to prevent losing our jobs.

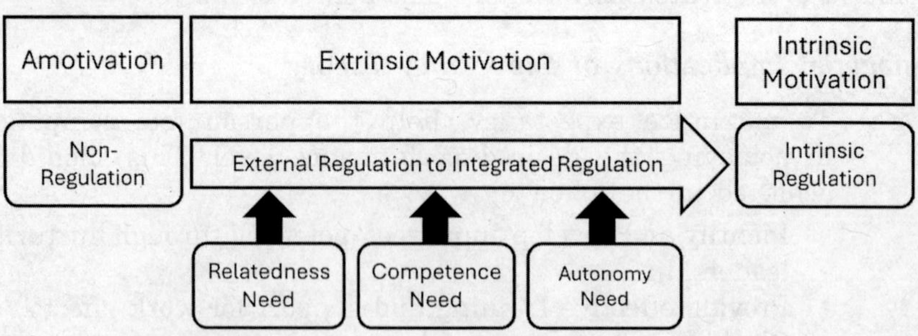

FIGURE 7.9 Self-Determination Theory of Motivation.

Figure 7.9 illustrates a condensed version of the Self-Determination Model developed by Ryan and Deci. This model suggests that people initially operate in an amotivational state. Amotivation differs from demotivation; instead, it is an emotional condition characterized by a complete lack of motivation. As individuals gradually align with their goals and processes, they adopt an extrinsic motivational state, shifting their drive from non-regulation to external regulation. The more involved we become in the process, the more our needs for relatedness, competence, and autonomy are satisfied. This progression leads us to transition from external regulation to integrated regulation. In integrated regulation, our efforts are fueled equally by both extrinsic and intrinsic sources.

When our needs for competence, relatedness, and autonomy are adequately met, and we begin to enjoy the process itself without concentrating on external rewards, intrinsic motivation is likely to arise. Consequently, people transition from an extrinsic to an intrinsic motivational state, where their efforts are self-regulated.

To motivate people, leaders design jobs and create policies that fulfill the needs for competence, relatedness, and autonomy. They avoid micromanaging their employees, allowing them to take ownership of their tasks. This approach enables employees to find solutions to problems, make decisions, and implement those solutions independently. Leaders provide essential training to their employees and celebrate their small wins to meet their need for competence and boost their confidence. Additionally, leaders create a collaborative and inclusive work environment that encourages peer recognition, allowing employees to feel valued and connected.

7.3.5 Csikszentmihalyi's Concept of Flow Experience

Csikszentmihalyi coined the term "flow experience" to describe a state where our intrinsic motivation is at its peak. This flow experience occurs when we become fully absorbed in tasks or activities that are both challenging and within our control. When we are in this state, we become so engaged in the task that we forget our worries and frustrations, leading to an altered perception of time; it can feel as though hours pass in mere minutes.

Our sense of self often disappears during a flow experience, and surprisingly, it reemerges as a stronger self after the task is completed. Flow experiences typically occur while engaging in activities such as watching movies or sports, playing games, reading books, listening to or playing music, and taking board exams.

Several key conditions are important for a flow experience to take place:

1. **Challenging Yet Achievable Task:** The task must be both challenging and achievable.
2. **Perceived Importance of Task:** The task's importance must be perceived as high, meaning it should be particularly significant for the person performing it.

3. **Utilization of a Variety of Skills:** When a person employs a range of skills to accomplish a task, a flow experience is more likely to occur.
4. **Autonomy for Making Choices:** Leaders must provide autonomy in making choices and offer immediate feedback to individuals performing the task.

The absence of challenge and skill variety, combined with strict management controls and rigid hierarchies, creates obstacles to achieving a flow experience. Leaders must set specific tasks that strike a balance between toughness and achievability, create a quiet workplace with minimal interruptions, and provide complete freedom to make choices.

7.3.6 Bandura's Social Cognitive Theory

Albert Bandura developed a Social Cognitive Theory of motivation based on his concept of Observational Learning, in which he suggested that people learn by watching and imitating the behavior, attitudes, and expressions of others. Observational learning occurs when certain conditions, such as attention, retention, reproduction, and motivation, are met. An individual must focus on the model's behavior, remember what they observed, have the ability to replicate the behavior, and have a reason to imitate it.

In his social cognitive theory, Bandura discovered that self-perception significantly affects motivation by enhancing or limiting it. People seek positive feedback about their abilities and are more likely to pursue goals they believe they can achieve. Bandura developed a valuable framework of three elements for understanding self-directed behavior within social cognitive theory, as shown in Figure 7.10.

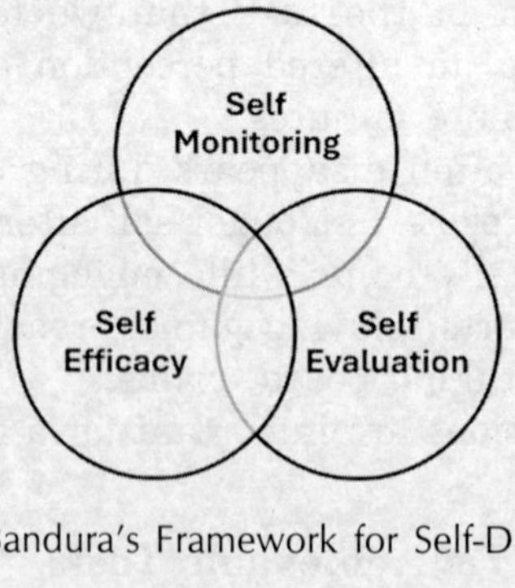

FIGURE 7.10 Bandura's Framework for Self-Directed Behavior.

1. **Self-Monitoring:** People use feedback from others to change their behavior.
2. **Self-Evaluation:** People compare their performance with their perception of competence. A belief in one's own high competence may lead to increased effort and motivation.

3. **Self-Efficacy:** Individuals believe they can effectively manage any specific situation. In other words, self-efficacy refers to the belief in one's own skills, competencies, and ability to accomplish tasks. People with high self-efficacy beliefs are motivated to put in their best efforts.

To apply social cognitive theory to induce motivation, leaders highlight the success stories of experienced employees as models to emulate. They promote knowledge-sharing sessions between successful seniors and newcomers. SCT theory posits that high self-efficacy in employees leads to better performance. To boost self-efficacy, leaders should provide training, give constructive feedback, celebrate small wins, encourage goal-setting, reinforce good performance, and foster a positive organizational climate. Effective leaders mentor employees to develop self-monitoring systems for self-directed behavior.

7.4 Demotivators

Many managers often carry out important activities incorrectly, creating a demotivating environment. As leaders, we should ensure that all activities are performed correctly and that any sources of demotivation are eliminated from the workplace. Common demotivators are listed below:

(a) **Performance evaluation:** Improper performance evaluation can lead to demotivation. Here are a few examples of its incorrect implementation:
- Employees feel uncertain about their roles in the workplace when performance evaluations are not conducted.
- Leaders and employees believe that performance evaluations are not beneficial and are carried out only for filing purposes.
- Managers use performance evaluations not as a means of feedback but rather as a tool to intimidate employees.
- Performance evaluations are sometimes seen as destructive sessions where employees are informed of their poor performance. This approach emphasizes avoiding rewards and minimizing organizational costs.

(b) **No Feedback:** Constructive feedback on performance acts as guidance for future improvement. It helps employees understand expectations, identify areas for enhancement, and offer clear steps to achieve those improvements. Without an effective feedback system, employees may struggle to perform well due to a lack of clarity in these aspects. Uncertainty regarding performance expectations is a significant source of demotivation.

(c) **Vague instructions:** Unclear job descriptions can make individuals feel inadequate, especially if they are unsure of what is expected of them.

(d) **No recognition:** The team will feel demotivated if they receive no recognition for a well-done job. Genuine acknowledgment inspires employees.

(e) **Recognition is given where it was not earned:** Recognizing the wrong person can demotivate other employees.

(f) **Role overload:** Too much work with insufficient time can lead to poor-quality results and decreased motivation.

(g) **Poor planning:** Poor planning results in time wastage, subpar performance, and demotivation.

(h) **Incompetence:** Employees who lack the knowledge to use equipment and are unwilling to learn become demotivated.

(i) **No Personal Development:** If there are no opportunities for creativity and innovation in the workplace, and employees cannot reach their full potential, demotivation occurs.

(j) **Poor and tense work environment:** Here are the symptoms of a poor and tense work environment that lead to demotivation:
- Colleagues with personal differences often engage in destructive criticism and exhibit disloyalty, gossip, and unfriendliness towards one another.
- Excessive rationalization for poor performance.
- Employees are not aware of the organization's vision and mission.
- Lack of leadership.
- Unchallenging and uninteresting tasks.
- Unjust leave system.
- There is a lack of teamwork and no established team goals.
- Lack of empowerment.

(k) **Bureaucracy:** The following are some key features of bureaucracy that can lead to demotivation among workers.
- There are too many rules, regulations, and excessive procedures.
- Over supervision.
- Lack of accountability.
- Delayed implementation of proposals.

7.5 The Role of Leaders in Enhancing Motivation

Earlier in this chapter, exploring motivational theories and innovative approaches to understanding motivation highlights several key elements that leaders must integrate into the organizational climate to promote motivation.

1. *Empower Employees with Full Autonomy and Control*

Motivation peaks when employees have complete control over specific tasks. They should be granted the freedom to decide what needs to be done, how it will be accomplished, and at what pace. In summary, they ought to have space for creativity and innovation. It allows employees to fully identify with their roles, which is rewarding and contributes to high productivity.

It indicates that a leader's role must shift from authoritarian to supportive. Leaders should refrain from interfering in daily activities. Their role changes to:

- Serving as a source of knowledge and experience.
- To coordinate and develop strategies for the future.
- To serve as both a role model and a coach.

The more individuals are empowered, the more responsibility they exhibit. A barrier to motivation arises when people are given responsibility without being empowered.

2. *Provide Opportunities for Learning*

Providing learning opportunities enables individuals to acquire new skills and grow. This, in turn, allows them to tackle more challenging tasks. The learning process itself is a rewarding experience. Meeting more demanding challenges by developing new skills can be profoundly motivating. The best results occur when skills and challenges are balanced. Learning refreshes individuals mentally, and fostering a culture of continuous learning enhances personal mastery and self-esteem. The more knowledge people possess, the broader the foundation they have for generating ideas and solving problems.

3. *Encourage Teamwork*

Being part of a team makes work more enjoyable and stimulating. A team provides a supportive environment for individuals. Team members can choose their own level of challenge, which is not fixed and can change depending on the situation. Additionally, team members are exposed to diversity, facilitating cross-training through exchanging skills and increased flexibility. This diversity makes work more interesting and enjoyable.

4. *Ensure a Positive Work Environment*

If we hear about internal conflicts or office politics that create an unpleasant work environment, remember that we have the power to address these issues as a leader. Listening and taking action demonstrate that we care about fostering a positive workplace.

5. *Management by Objective*

Managers and employees should work together to set specific goals and action plans to achieve the organization's objectives. It is essential to allow open input from employees during this process. We can organize the discussion into the following topic areas:

- Performance goals and objectives
- Skills and knowledge development
- Processes and methods
- Feedback

6. *Participative Management*

Employee participation encourages greater dedication to the organization's success. One example is a program in which employees can acquire stock in the company as part of their benefits. Another is the establishment of self-directed teams.

7. *Job Enrichment and Redesign*

Forming natural workgroups can help employees better understand their roles within the organization's overall structure. Additionally, combining tasks to increase variety may enhance the sense of meaning in their work, which could boost motivation.

8. *Modified Work Schedule*

It allows employees to adjust their schedules according to their needs, such as working flexible hours and enabling some or all of their work to be done outside of traditional office settings (referred to as Virtual Offices).

9. *Provide Training Opportunities*

Today, employees generally view employer-sponsored training as a valuable opportunity. They appreciate any workplace training they receive, as it helps them build their skills and enhances their job security. However, in today's high-tech world, offering various development opportunities, including online learning, traditional classroom training, and on-the-job skill development, is essential. It is especially true for younger employees, who may be tempted to leave an organization if they feel their potential is not fully utilized.

10. *Provide on-the-job Coaching*

Coaching has been recognized as a key factor in employees' success for many years. All employees appreciate a genuine pat on the back, which is an inexpensive and effective retention tool for most companies. However, coaching involves much more than just offering flattery or empty praise. As a coach, we teach employees and provide specific feedback on their performance. Individual attention is crucial for making employees feel valued and enhancing their performance. Mentoring is another effective method to help employees develop the skills and experience needed to succeed. Ultimately, nothing motivates employees more than achieving success!

11. *Provide a Challenging Work*

The most credible research on motivation from the past 50 years demonstrates that employees are primarily motivated by their work itself, while other factors are less significant. Jobs don't have to be routine, dull, or demotivating. Various job redesign strategies can help renew employees' interest and rekindle their enthusiasm. Introducing new tasks, projects, and responsibilities can make employees' roles more challenging and engaging. If we don't try to stretch our team, we risk losing them.

12. *Cultivate an Atmosphere of Respect*

Employees from all generations do not respond well to feeling like just another number, a mere cog in the wheel, or an invisible part of the organization. It is essential for all employees to feel that their efforts are recognized and genuinely appreciated. The issue goes beyond simply being flexible, providing feedback, or creating meaningful tasks. Respecting our employees' needs, acknowledging their individuality, and offering fair opportunities are essential. When employees feel valued, they are more likely to appreciate their ongoing employment with the company.

All strategies are based on established principles and can only succeed if employees are empowered to make decisions without external control. Ultimately, each department within a company should operate like a mini-business, with employees taking complete control and responsibility for their work. Therefore, mutual trust is essential.

7.6 A Refreshing Approach to Motivation

When companies want to change their customers' purchasing behavior, they rely on the expertise of advertising agencies to persuade them. However, when they want to change the behavior of their employees in a specific direction, they call it motivation. (Hershey 1993).

Hershey believes managers can persuade employees to perform specific tasks, but this is not the same as motivation. Motivation can occur after persuasion, especially when the employee finds the desired behavior appealing.

Employers should focus on understanding the psychology of advertising rather than solely relying on theories of motivation. Effective communication is crucial for persuasive techniques. Robert Hershey believes that the persuasion strategies used by marketing departments can serve as valuable motivational tools. The following approaches should be considered:

- Expert opinions are persuasive; influential figures can enhance our argument.
- Testimonials from trustworthy and credible employees are more believable.
- **Logos:** Repeated messaging enhances audience engagement and recall of the message. Multiple independent sources that support the same idea have proven to be effective. Real-world examples or case studies are often more persuasive than statistics.
- **Pathos:** Eliciting emotions such as happiness, sadness, or anger can strengthen our argument.
- **Ethos:** If people have faith in us and trust us, we are more likely to persuade them.

Hershey offers a refreshing perspective, and it may be beneficial for companies to consider using the same persuasive techniques employed in advertising to encourage desirable behavior among employees. Motivation could become significantly more straightforward if employees can be motivated this way, as persuasion can foster belief. People will do a lot for money, more for a good leader, but they will do the most for what they believe in. Hershey's perspective certainly has merits and deserves further investigation.

7.7 Spiritual Dimensions in Motivation

According to Maslow's hierarchy of needs theory (1943), satisfying lower-order needs—such as food, clothing, shelter, and security—is crucial for motivating workers. Once these basic needs are met, individuals typically move towards higher-order needs, such as self-esteem and self-actualization.

However, this progression does not always occur as expected. People with high salaries and elevated status often seek fulfillment and satisfaction primarily through possessions such as money, property, gold, and cars. Consequently, they become increasingly fearful of losing these material possessions. In contrast, a poorly paid school teacher, a self-employed artisan, or a priest may demonstrate a higher level of self-actualization despite having lower satisfaction with their basic needs.

This situation can be understood through the theory of "self-transcendence" as described in the Bhagavad Gita (Prabhupada, 2003).

According to this theory, a person who embraces graciousness and surrenders their greed, envy, egotism, and desire for status at the feet of Lord Krishna while nurturing a sense of contribution and integrity achieves a state of transcendence.

A person in the self-transcendence stage is free from endless needs and desires. They understand that their existence means not fulfilling personal desires but contributing to society by acquiring and sharing knowledge and striving for excellence in their work.

Individuals who reach self-transcendence are willing to sacrifice their lower-order needs for higher goals. They find satisfaction and peace of mind through a sense of contribution and service. Therefore, their motivation stems from acts of sacrifice rather than personal gratification and from charity instead of acquisition.

The sense of service and contribution significantly influences the depth and sustainability of our happiness, satisfaction, and peace of mind. For instance, imagine living alone on an island and receiving a letter of appreciation from the head of our country for our good work. While we may initially experience a brief moment of happiness upon receiving the letter, that feeling will quickly fade because there is no one with whom to share our success. As a result, the depth of our happiness and satisfaction will be minimal.

Further, imagine we are working at a company and, due to our excellent performance, we receive a promotion and a salary increase. We feel happy and satisfied for a day or so, sharing our achievements with colleagues, friends, and family members who congratulate us. However, after that initial excitement, our achievement becomes a past event, and the intensity of our happiness and satisfaction begins to fade.

When we are a part of a successful team, we share the joy with all team members. This collective experience of happiness can be enjoyed repeatedly, sustaining our joy for an extended period and amplifying our motivation. Consequently, group success is more significant than individual success.

Consider the importance of contribution and service. Suppose our team engages in meaningful activities for society. In that case, the entire community or country will benefit from our team's success, resulting in profound and lasting happiness and satisfaction. This sense of fulfillment and peace of mind will also be sustainable. Therefore, as true leaders, we must instill this sense of contribution and service in our subordinates and integrate it into our organizational culture. This approach will foster enduring happiness, satisfaction, and peace of mind, ultimately leading to self-transcendence and organizational transcendence.

ASSESSMENTS

1. With suitable examples, explain Herzberg's two-factor theory of motivation.
2. Describe the job characteristics model developed by Hackman and Oldham.
3. Explain the goal-setting motivational theory and describe how you will apply this theory to motivate your employees.
4. Explain the equity theory of motivation and how you would implement this theory within your organization.

CHAPTER 8

Empowerment

8.1 Empowerment

Empowerment is the process of enhancing the capacity of individuals or groups through education, access to resources, a supportive environment, and the delegation of power, enabling them to make choices and translate those choices into desired actions and outcomes. When employees are properly empowered, they become more motivated to complete tasks efficiently and effectively. It is essential to trust our employees and embrace their imperfections to make them empowered. Empowered individuals are more engaged in their work, willing to tackle challenging tasks, and approach their responsibilities with confidence.

The common perception among managers regarding empowerment is that it simply involves delegating authority to make choices and decisions, essentially sharing power with frontline employees. However, this understanding is insufficient for achieving true empowerment. In order to design an effective empowerment program, it is crucial to determine the information that should be communicated to employees, provide them with the required knowledge, skills, and competencies for independent decision-making and action, and motivate them through suitable recognition and rewards.

8.2 Bowen and Lawler's Empowerment Model

Figure 8.1 illustrates an empowerment model developed by Bowen and Lawler in 1995.

Bowen and Lawler defined empowerment as the practice of sharing four key organizational elements with front-line employees: Power, Information, Knowledge, and Rewards. They suggest that empowerment occurs when organizations implement the practice of sharing these

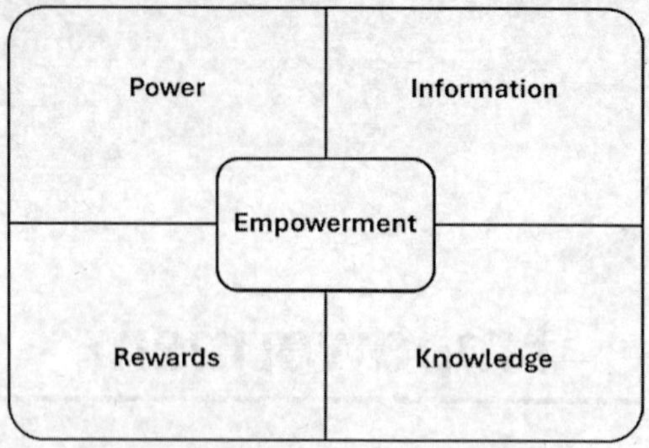

FIGURE 8.1 Bowen and Lawler Empowerment Model.

four elements with employees at all levels. Leaders utilize this model to empower employees, enhancing performance, job satisfaction, and customer service. This model is referred to as a multiplicative model in which all the elements interact by multiplying together, represented by the following equation:

$$\text{Power} \times \text{Information} \times \text{Knowledge} \times \text{Rewards} = \text{Empowerment}$$

The empowerment equation indicates that if any one of these elements is zero, the overall empowerment will also be zero.

Leadership Implications of the Bowen and Lawler Empowerment Model

Many managers pay lip service to the idea of employee empowerment. They often tell their teams that they are encouraged to approach tasks in their own way. However, in practice, these managers are hesitant to delegate authority, share information, or promote the development of their employees' knowledge and skills. Employees will not feel empowered by this empty rhetoric.

To effectively implement this empowerment model, leaders must adjust organizational policies, practices, and structures to foster and sustain empowerment. They need to establish a company-wide ecosystem that promotes the delegation of power to employees at every level.

This facilitates independent decision-making by sharing information, enhancing employees' knowledge and skills, and creating a robust system for recognizing and rewarding exceptional performance.

Recognizing and rewarding employee performance reinforces the importance of empowerment while motivating employees. Sharing information involves the organization's vision, mission, and strategies, available resources, performance standards, and customer feedback.

8.3 Spreitzer's Psychological Empowerment Model

As illustrated in Figure 8.2, the Psychological Empowerment Model developed by Gretchen Spreitzer focuses on the psychological aspects of

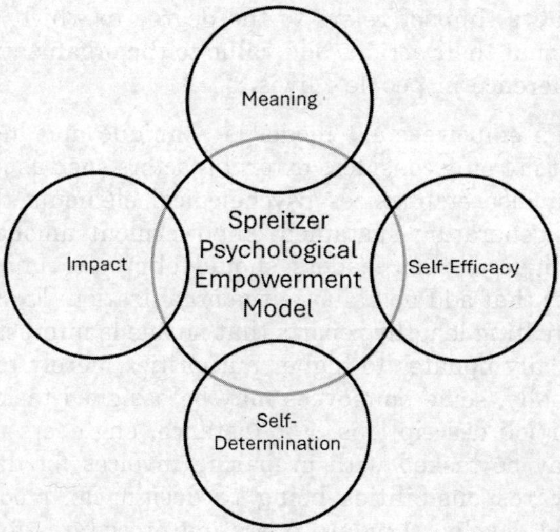

FIGURE 8.2 Spreitzer Psychological Empowerment Model.

empowerment. It explains how employees feel empowered by perceiving their roles and capabilities. This model identifies four psychological dimensions that, when perceived positively, promote psychological empowerment. The four dimensions are explained as follows:

1. **Meaning:** Meaning refers to the value that employees assign to their tasks. Employees view a task as more valuable if it enhances their sense of purpose. People evaluate tasks based on their own values and standards. For example, if a teacher is asked to write a book, they may see this task as highly valuable because they believe it is an important part of their career. In contrast, if they are asked to simply maintain files in the office, they are likely to assign significantly less value to this task, as they do not consider it a significant part of their professional life.
2. **Self-Efficacy:** Self-efficacy refers to the belief in one's ability to perform a specific task. When a task aligns with an individual's skills and competencies, they often feel confident about successfully completing it, which fosters a sense of empowerment. Conversely, if the task does not match their skills, they may feel demotivated. For example, if a carpentry job is assigned to an electrician, they will likely feel demotivated due to a lack of skills required for carpentry work.
3. **Self-Determination:** When employees perceive their assigned jobs as meaningful and aligned with their skill sets, and when they are given appropriate autonomy in their work, they become intrinsically motivated to perform, generating a strong sense of empowerment.

4. **Impact:** Impact refers to the degree to which an individual feels that their actions add value to the organization and make a difference in people's lives.

Spreitzer's empowerment model is a unique and highly effective approach, as it not only considers external factors such as job design and leadership but also emphasizes psychological elements that are more influential in generating sustained empowerment among individuals. This model suggests that leaders should eliminate unnecessary and redundant jobs that add no value to the organization. Examples of such jobs include creating lengthy reports that no one is interested in reading or providing daily updates to higher authorities merely to satisfy their egos. Additionally, some employees may be assigned tasks that do not relate to their job descriptions. For instance, engineers at automobile companies may be tasked with preparing invoices for dealers despite their primary responsibilities being to design car models, optimize workflows, and develop standard operating procedures for shop floors.

Leaders must ensure that the jobs assigned to employees are meaningful to them and impactful for the organization. They must provide employees with autonomy for decision-making and job performance. Additionally, they must arrange necessary training programs to enhance the skills and competencies of their employees. If the Spreitzer Empowerment model is appropriately applied in the organizational environment, it will exceptionally enhance organizational productivity.

Zappos and the Spreitzer Empowerment Model

Zappos is an e-commerce company that sells shoes, clothing, handbags, and accessories. It is headquartered in Las Vegas, Nevada, and is renowned for its exceptional customer service and culture. To increase employee engagement and retention, facilitate faster decision-making and innovation, and enhance customer satisfaction and brand loyalty, the company adopted 'Holacracy.' Holacracy is a system that replaces traditional hierarchical structures with distributed decision-making. Proper implementation of Holacracy requires genuine empowerment of employees. To achieve employee empowerment, the company adopted the Spreitzer Empowerment Model. The following were their implementation strategies:

- **Meaning:** Employees were emotionally aligned with the company's mission to deliver exceptional happiness to customers through innovation, quality products, faster decision-making, and positive employee behavior.
- **Self-Efficacy:** The company heavily invested in technical and behavioral training for employees to enhance their knowledge and skills.

- **Self-Determination:** The company's Holacracy model allowed employees to take initiative and make faster decisions without much interference from managers. Employee autonomy improved customer satisfaction.
- **Impact:** Ultimately, employees recognized that their initiatives, quicker decision-making, and innovative ideas were creating exceptional happiness for their customers. They began readily sharing innovative ideas to enhance products and processes.

Spreitzer's Empowerment Model and Holacracy system brought tremendous success to Zappos, making employees motivated, capable, and impactful.

8.4 Why Does Employee Empowerment Fail?

In addition to the reasons for empowerment failure outlined in Bowen and Lawler's Empowerment Model, there are three additional significant reasons for empowerment failures, as illustrated in Figure 8.3.

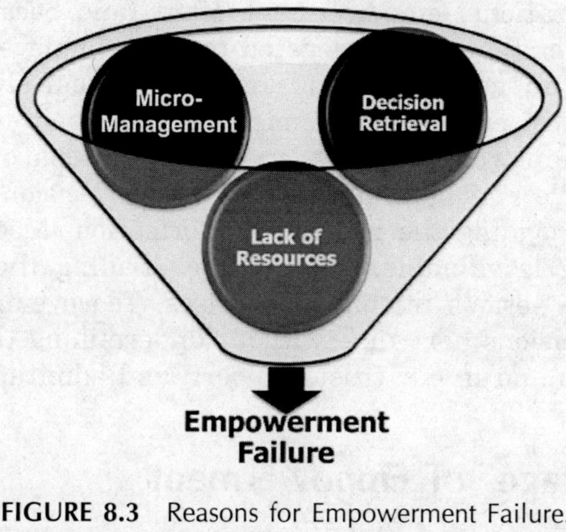

FIGURE 8.3 Reasons for Empowerment Failure.

1. *Micromanagement*

Managers define decision-making authority and set boundaries for their staff, but they often micromanage their work. They want to know every action their employees take and require them to submit daily reports detailing all activities on the ground. As a result, employees become so occupied with preparing these lengthy reports that they neglect other important tasks. This behavior typically stems from a lack of trust in their staff's ability to make sound decisions.

An HR manager extended the company's hiring process by ten days because he insisted on signing every document involved. As a result, the paperwork often sat on his desk for days without action since staff were instructed not to proceed without his signature. His lack of trust undermined the concept of employee empowerment. Do employees make mistakes? Absolutely, but misleading them about their boundaries is far worse.

2. *Lack of Resources*

Merely delegating power to employees is insufficient; we must provide them with the necessary resources to work both efficiently and effectively. For instance, as an army officer at the border, we are authorized to make decisions during wartime, yet our unit cannot survive for long without a consistent supply of ammunition, food, medical services, and technological support. In the same way, employees in a business organization need essential resources like machinery, funding, materials, and advanced technology.

3. *Decision Retrieval*

In most organizations, empowerment often fails because managers reclaim the power they have delegated to their employees. While they may be willing to make numerous mistakes themselves, they tend to be intolerant of even a single mistake from their team members. For genuine empowerment, it's crucial to accept our employees' imperfections. We can help staff make sound decisions by coaching, training, and providing the necessary information. Modeling effective decision-making is valuable, but avoid overriding their empowered choices unless a serious complication arises. Teach employees how to make better decisions next time without undermining their confidence in their abilities and in our trust, support, and admiration.

8.5 Advantages of Empowerment

There are several benefits of empowerment for employees, organizations, and customers, which are outlined below:

1. *Advantages of Empowerment for Employees*

Empowerment addresses the higher needs of individuals, which in turn leads to increased job satisfaction and motivation, a greater sense of ownership and responsibility, and improved skills and career development. Research shows that individuals require self-efficacy to excel in life, which is the belief in one's capacity to produce results or outcomes. Empowerment helps eliminate conditions that lead to powerlessness while boosting employees' sense of self-efficacy. It also enables employees to manage situations and gives them the ability to take control of problems as they arise.

Most people join an organization with the desire to do a good job, and empowerment helps to harness their inherent motivation. Empowerment acts as an intrinsic reward for employees, providing them with a sense of personal mastery and competence.

2. *Advantages of Empowerment for Organizations*

Empowerment enhances the overall strength of an organization. In simple terms, when everyone in the organization possesses power, the organization becomes more resilient. Freedom from excessive control allows subordinates to utilize their talents and abilities, resulting in higher employee retention rates, reduced turnover, and increased adaptability in a turbulent business environment.

Empowered employees engage more deeply in their work. Leaders can focus more on strategic issues because empowered employees handle daily challenges effectively.

The product life cycle has significantly shortened in today's rapidly changing technological landscape and shifting customer preferences. As a result, organizations must accelerate their research and innovation processes to develop new products and enhance existing ones. Organizations can foster innovation by empowering their subordinates and improving their responsiveness to the markets they serve.

3. *Advantages of Employee Empowerment for Customers*

When employees are empowered to make decisions, they no longer have to seek approval from managers. This shortens response time, enabling customers to receive quicker solutions to their problems. They benefit from improved service experiences due to personalized and responsive interactions with empowered employees.

8.6 Beyond Empowerment: Sense of Ownership

Today, leaders are encouraging employees to develop a sense of ownership in their work. Employees who feel this ownership tend to approach their tasks with an owner's mindset.

Organizations frequently allocate company stock to their employees to cultivate a sense of ownership. However, these small stock allocations often fail to create genuine ownership, as many employees opt to sell their shares in the market once they realize a profit. The sense of ownership is more psychological than financial. Let us explore what happens when employees adopt a worker's mindset or vice versa.

8.6.1 Employees with Worker's Mindset

Employees with a worker's mindset worry about how their superiors perceive their actions. They tend to protect their functional areas and pursue their self-interests. They feel compelled to adhere to the rules, even when those rules contradict common sense. While rules are important for maintaining an organization's integrity, common sense is crucial in certain situations, and we may need to make decisions that go against the rules.

Employees with a worker mindset focus mainly on compensation, recognition, and rewards tied to their performance. They feel satisfied when they perform well and receive suitable rewards. These workers are comfortable being managed by their supervisors and value being monitored. However, they often avoid taking risks or initiating new ideas, knowing that they will have to provide a written explanation in case of failure.

8.6.2 Employees with Owner's Mindset

Employees with an owner's mindset prioritize the business outcomes of their actions, regardless of who is observing them. They are willing to bend, stretch, or even break rules that contradict common sense. They are unafraid to make risky decisions and take initiative because they feel responsible for helping the organization grow. These individuals act without waiting for direction from their superiors; they refuse to be mere spectators. They understand it is up to them to take action, as no one else will do it. They would never consider leaving the organization, even in their dreams, because they see their workplace as an extension of their family. They view the organization as their home, which they are committed to protecting at all costs.

8.6.3 How to Foster a Sense of Ownership?

In order to foster a sense of ownership among employees, it is essential to align them with the organization's vision. Leaders should trust their employees' abilities and share organizational information with them. Additionally, we should encourage our employees to participate in both strategic and organizational decision-making processes.

We should empower employees to manage resources independently, accepting that they might make mistakes and allowing them the 'freedom to fail.' This philosophy involves allocating funds to potentially risky projects, providing employees with confidence, and learning opportunities.

By providing adequate mentorship, we help our employees address their limitations and imperfections. In a self-reporting system, leaders should motivate employees to evaluate their own initiatives and actions. As leaders, our role is to discuss the outcomes with our employees and prompt them to identify their own solutions if any gaps or issues arise.

ASSESSMENTS

1. Explain the Bowen and Lawler empowerment model.
2. Define psychological empowerment. How will you apply Spreitzer's psychological empowerment model within your organization?
3. Differentiate between the worker's mindset and the employer's mindset.

CHAPTER 9

Building High-Performance Teams

9.1 Teams

Empowering employees as individuals or groups will not make much of a difference unless they are empowered as a team. It is a reality of organizational life that one can rarely succeed alone, no matter how competent or empowered one may be. Teams consistently outperform individuals acting alone, especially when performance requires diverse skills, judgments, and experiences. Today, high-performing teams are the mantra for success in business organizations.

A team consists of enthusiastic individuals dedicated to achieving shared objectives, collaborating effectively, and delivering high-quality outcomes. According to Katzenbach and Smith (1993), "A team is a small number of people with complementary skills who are committed to a common purpose, a common approach, and performance goals for which they hold themselves mutually accountable." In any situation that requires the real-time combination of multiple skills, experiences, and judgments, a team undoubtedly produces better results than a collection of empowered individuals operating within confined job roles and responsibilities. This blend of skills and experiences allows teams to address multifaceted challenges such as innovation, quality, and customer service.

9.2 Group Vs. Team

People often think of a team as a collection of individuals working independently to achieve personal and organizational objectives. In organizations, employees are grouped together for administrative convenience. However, a true team is more than just a collection of individuals. A team consists of people who unite to collaborate and achieve a shared goal for which they hold each other mutually accountable. Team members rely heavily on one another, demonstrating a high level of interdependence. In contrast, individuals in a group work independently to accomplish their personal goals.

A team is a group of people with a high degree of interdependence, focused on achieving a common goal. Team members are deeply committed to each other's personal growth and success. This commitment often extends beyond the team. A team surpasses a group and exceeds all reasonable expectations placed on its members; in other words, it creates a synergistic effect—one plus one equals eleven, not two. Exhibit 9.1 illustrates the key differences between a group and a team.

EXHIBIT 9.1 Key Differences between a Group and a Team

Group	Team
1. A group has a designated strong leader.	Leadership roles are shared in a team.
2. A group can consist of many people.	A team essentially consists of a small number of people.
3. No consensus on a common approach.	A consensus on a common approach is consciously generated.
4. The missions of the group and the organization are similar.	The team has an explicit mission.
5. Individuals are solely responsible and accountable for their own tasks.	Shared responsibility and accountability for achieving the team's goals.
6. Group performance reflects the sum of individual performances.	Team members perform collectively.
7. The hierarchical structure is prominent, and individual accountabilities differ.	Horizontal structure is prominent, and individual accountabilities are similar.
8. Feedback flows from higher positions to lower positions.	Reciprocal feedback, open discussions, and proactive problem-solving.
9. The commitment of personal relationships among group members varies, often within the organization's boundaries.	Commitment in personal relationships among team members is similar and transcends organizational boundaries.
10. Each individual's skills may differ, but they do not necessarily complement others' skills for achieving shared goals.	An individual's skills complement those of others to achieve shared goals.

9.3 Advantages of Team

A high-performance team could provide four significant advantages to the organization:

1. **It maximizes the organization's human resources.**
Each team member is coached, supported, and guided by the others. All members experience success or failure, not just the individual. Failures are not attributed to individual members, which gives them the courage to take risks and take initiative. Success is shared by every team member, helping them to set and achieve larger and better goals. Moreover, failure is viewed as a learning opportunity.
2. **There are superior outputs against all odds.**
This is due to the synergistic effect of a team; a team can typically outperform a group of individuals.
3. **There is continuous improvement.**
No one understands the job, tasks, and goals better than the individual team members. To achieve real change, we need their knowledge, skills, and abilities. When they unite as a team, they will not hesitate to demonstrate their capabilities. Personal motives will be set aside to prioritize the team's success.
4. **Generate extraordinary performance.**
The presence of high-performance teams across all levels of the organization transforms an average organization into a high-performing one, fostering exceptional performance.

9.4 Team Fundamentals

As leaders, we can build an effective team by emphasizing the fundamentals of teamwork, as illustrated in Figure 9.1.

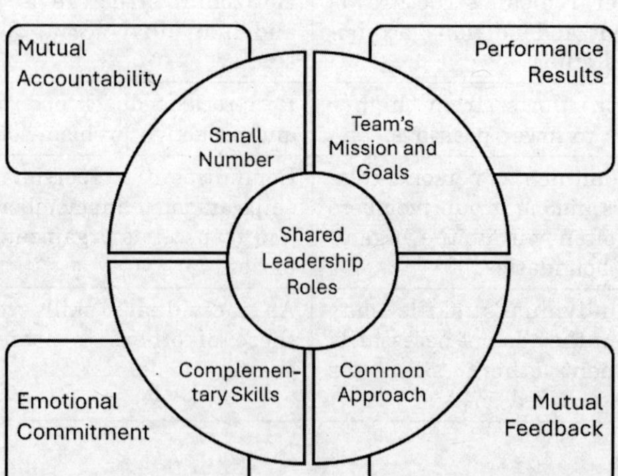

FIGURE 9.1 Team Fundamentals.

1. *Shared Leadership Roles*

Effective team leaders understand that their primary goal is to achieve results collaboratively rather than focusing solely on individual accomplishments, including their own. They recognize that they don't have all the answers, so they avoid insisting on leading the team alone. As a result, leadership roles are rotated based on the context and situation.

2. *Small Number*

If a team consists of a large number of individuals, they struggle to interact constructively. A smaller number is more effective for working productively with a common approach, complementary skills, and mutual accountability. The ideal team size should be between 2 and 15 members. A larger group, perhaps fifty or more, can theoretically form a team, but such large groups are more likely to break into sub-teams rather than function as a single unit.

3. *Team's Mission and Goals*

To transform a regular team into a high-performing one, leaders empower and support team members in independently developing their team's mission and goals. Leaders make sure that each team member actively participates in creating the team's mission and goals. This exercise fosters commitment among team members to their team's mission and goals.

4. *Consensus on a Common Approach*

Once the team has established its mission and goals, it is time for the members to develop a unified strategy to achieve them collaboratively. Team members need to agree on several key aspects, including who will handle specific tasks, how schedules will be created and followed, which skills should be enhanced, the expected conduct of each team member, and the criteria and approach for making or modifying decisions. This includes determining when and how to adjust their strategy to complete the tasks. It is essential to reach an agreement on the details of the work and how it integrates individual skills and development, as this fosters commitment to a unified approach.

5. *Complementary Skills*

It is essential to acknowledge the significance of complementary skills when forming a team. A team cannot begin without a variety of skills that enhance one another, particularly in technical and problem-solving areas. To achieve its goals, a team must cultivate the diverse skills necessary for success. Thus, a team needs to possess the right mix of complementary skills, ensuring that all required abilities are present to reach its objectives.

For example, in a marketing team at a product-based organization, it is essential to have individuals with a diverse range of skills. This includes technical expertise, sales proficiency, mass communication abilities for advertising, logistics knowledge, and IT specialists, among others. If a team consists exclusively of salespeople, they may struggle in areas that require mass communication and IT skills. In order to attain excellence and thrive in the marketplace, it is essential to assemble a team of experts from diverse disciplines who can effectively leverage each other's strengths.

6. *Mutual Accountability*

No group ever becomes a team until it can hold itself accountable as a unit. At its core, team accountability revolves around the genuine promises we make to ourselves and others regarding our responsibility for the team's goals and performance outcomes. Trust is a crucial element in fostering mutual accountability among team members. Members must adopt proactive habits, as proactive individuals recognize their duty to take the initiative in achieving the team's mission and goals while also holding themselves accountable for the results.

7. *Excellent Performance Results*

In the final examination, performance serves as both the cause and effect of team success. Beyond specific and tangible performance outcomes, everything else holds minimal significance. To determine whether a particular group is a true team, examine its performance results first.

8. *Mutual Feedback from Team Members*

Mutual feedback among team members is more genuine and transparent. It encourages the development of feedforward for future performance, enabling earlier mistakes to be corrected. It is not meant to administer rewards or penalties. Its only purpose is to ensure improved performance next time.

9. *Emotional Commitment to Each Other*

High-performing teams distinguish themselves from regular teams through a profound emotional commitment among their members. This commitment extends well beyond basic courtesies and teamwork; it persists even after the team has disbanded. It encompasses more than just having close-knit relationships; it embodies each individual's strong dedication to supporting one another's growth, progress, and success.

Fueled by this heightened sense of interpersonal commitment, the team's purpose becomes more meaningful to its members. They begin to perceive one member's failure as their own, fostering mutual concern for each other's growth and development. This culture encourages the development of transferable skills and enhances flexibility within the team.

In high-performing teams, leadership roles are shared and rotated more easily than in typical teams. Members demonstrate a stronger sense of contribution, along with humor and enjoyment in their work.

9.5 Leader's Role in Building a High-Performance Team

To build a high-performing team within the organization, leaders emphasize the key elements of team building outlined in Exhibit 9.2.

EXHIBIT 9.2 Essential Elements of Team Building	
1.	Careful selection of team members.
2.	Clearly define the team's mission together.
3.	Establishing practical teamwork norms.
4.	Build consensus for a common approach.
5.	Encourage the use of jargon.
6.	Encourage cooperation.
7.	Celebrate small wins.
8.	Emphasize mutual feedback.
9.	Provide autonomy to the entire team.
10.	Assess the genuineness of the team.

1. *Careful Selection of Team Members*

Choosing unqualified individuals for a team will inevitably lead to failure, no matter how much effort we invest. As leaders, we must carefully choose team members based on their skills and character. Certain essential characteristics are necessary to qualify as a member of a high-performing team, which are outlined below:

- **Integrity:** A person must be honest, ethical, and transparent in all interactions. He should treat all teammates with respect.
- **Communication Skills:** All selected team members should have excellent communication skills, including active listening, clear communication, and the ability to provide constructive feedback.
- **Inclusivity:** Team members must respect diverse perspectives and actively contribute to a collaborative environment. They should address disagreements professionally and collaborate to find mutually beneficial solutions.

- **Proactive:** Team members must be eager to take initiative, work consistently, and strive for high-quality results.
- **Confidentiality:** Team members must handle sensitive information with care and ensure that confidentiality is maintained as necessary.

2. *Carefully Define the Team's Mission Together*

Leaders should encourage team members to actively participate in creating the team's mission. The mission must address a specific purpose for the team, a clear goal, and a philosophical tone. Commitment from team members to the team's mission will provide a solid foundation for a high-performing team. It will also provide emotional anchorage to team members and assist them in making relevant decisions. The leaders must establish a climate in which team members can freely express their feelings, ideas, and opinions.

3. *Establishing Practical Teamwork Norms*

A norm is a standard of conduct that is shared among team members and guides their behavior. Leaders play a crucial role in shaping the team's cultural values and norms, defining the boundaries of acceptable behavior, and providing a reference for what is considered right or wrong. To establish various teamwork norms, leaders encourage team members to treat one another as if they were customers, promoting cooperative behavior and politeness.

Norms can be either documented or developed as unwritten understandings over time. Newly formed teams often find it practical to start with an initial set of norms, understanding that these will need to be reviewed and modified regularly. Some teams choose to revisit their norms at the beginning or end of each meeting. Establishing and adhering to team norms helps build discipline, fosters trust among team members, and supports a safe environment. Exhibit 9.3 provides examples of teamwork norms.

4. *Build Consensus for a Common Approach*

To achieve a higher level of performance, all team members need to adopt a unified approach to completing tasks. Leaders should encourage team members to participate in developing a shared strategy. They can guide the team in building consensus through group discussions. This unified approach offers consistent guidelines that help team members create synergy within the environment.

5. *Encouraging the use of Jargon*

Jargon is a specialized language that fosters cohesion and commitment, forming strong bonds among team members. It reinforces unique

EXHIBIT 9.3 Sample Teamwork Norms	
1.	Treat one another with dignity and respect.
2.	Transparency: Be transparent and open; avoid hidden agendas.
3.	Be genuine with each other about ideas, challenges, and feelings.
4.	Please trust one another and have confidence that the matters discussed will remain confidential.
5.	It is essential to listen attentively to understand others and remain open to their input without being dismissive.
6.	Avoid being defensive when interacting with your colleagues.
7.	Instead of seeking out blame, extend understanding to your colleagues; adopt a clean slate approach.
8.	Let us support one another and avoid undermining each other.
9.	Avoid being territorial; instead, focus on the overall benefit to the company, your employees, and your customers.
10.	The discussion of issues, ideas, and direction should remain constructive and avoid devolving into personal attacks that could have future repercussions.
11.	It is okay not to have the correct answer, so admit it. The team can find the answer.
12.	Problems are presented in a manner that encourages mutual discussion and resolution.

values and significantly contributes to developing a high-performance organizational culture. By using jargon, team members can communicate more effectively, resulting in fewer misunderstandings.

6. *Encourage Cooperation*

Many managers mistakenly promote competition among team members, believing that competitive reward schemes will motivate their employees. However, this inner competition creates one winner and many losers. How can a team succeed against competitors if it includes so many losers? Instead, it is essential to introduce group reward schemes that foster cooperation among team members. When rewards are given for group accomplishments, they encourage collaboration and strengthen teamwork, as individuals are recognized for their collective efforts.

It is also important to recognize the contributions of outstanding performers. The team should present an award to highlight an exceptional contributor, which can further enhance teamwork and inspire others to excel.

7. *Celebrate Small Wins*

The number of tasks needed to accomplish the team's mission is substantial. It is crucial to inspire team members to sustain momentum continually. To cultivate this psychological energy, leaders celebrate small task achievements through tea sessions, coffee gatherings, team dinners, and brief trips to exotic locations.

8. *Emphasize Mutual Feedback*

The team should collaboratively assess and evaluate its performance. It can discuss areas for improvement and devise strategies to enhance its performance.

9. *Provide Autonomy to the Entire Team*

Micromanagers often lack trust in their employees' abilities and impose excessive control over their work. They tend to retain decision-making power for themselves and frequently interfere with their subordinates' daily activities. This constant oversight can inhibit the team's performance. As leaders, it is essential to adopt a macro-manager approach, trusting our employees and providing them with autonomy. We should allow our team members to manage their tasks and make independent daily decisions.

10. *Assess the Genuineness of the Team*

To work effectively on team fundamentals and build a cohesive team as a leader in a real-world setting, we need to assess the authenticity of our team by asking ourselves several questions and seeking the answers. The questions are compiled in Exhibit 9.4. Answering these questions can establish the extent to which our group operates as a true team and help identify ways to enhance our efforts to improve performance. They set high expectations, and meeting them can be a greater challenge than we realize. However, confronting the answers can accelerate our progress in realizing our team's full potential.

EXHIBIT 9.4 Questions to Assess the Genuineness of the Team
1. Does our team consist of a limited number of people? • Can team members quickly build mutual relationships and communicate with each other? • Is there a sufficient number of people to form sub-teams? • Do team members understand one another's nature, strengths, and weaknesses?
2. Does our team possess all the essential skills? • Are the team members prepared to learn various skills?
3. Are our team members in agreement about a common approach? • Is the approach meticulous and understood by every team member? • Is it developed collaboratively?

(Contd.)

4. Does our team possess a clearly defined team's mission? • Does it contribute to achieving the organizational mission? • Do all members understand and believe in the team's mission? • Are all members committed to the team's mission? • Do all members consult the mission before making strategic decisions?
5. Are the team's goals clearly defined and aligned with the team's mission? • Are they clear, direct, and measurable? • Are they defined mutually by team members?
6. Do our team members share a sense of responsibility and accountability? • Is there mutual trust in the environment? • Do all members understand their responsibility to take the initiative? • Do all members feel accountable for the results?

Google's Project Aristotle

In 2012, Google launched Project Aristotle to analyze 180 teams and determine the characteristics that make a team highly effective. Through Project Aristotle, Google identified five key characteristics of high-performing teams, which are elucidated as follows:

1. **Psychological Safety:** Team members should feel safe to take the initiative and voice their concerns. Mutual trust must exist among all team members. Google encouraged team leaders to foster mutual trust and maintain transparent communication among team members.
2. **Dependability:** High-performing teams depend on all members to attain performance results. It centers on cohesive team performance, as one person or a few individuals cannot produce the desired outcomes. Google introduced team norms that include consensus on a common approach, as well as mutual responsibility and accountability.
3. **Structure and Clarity:** Each team member must understand their roles, goals, and the team's mission. Google empowers team members to define their mission, objectives, and the roles and goals of each individual.
4. **Meaning:** Employees perform better when they understand how their achievements add value to their organization and society as a whole. Google requests team leaders to align the team's mission with organizational objectives and societal goals. They must inform team members about their valuable contributions to the organization and society.
5. **Impact:** Each team member wants to assess how their efforts contribute to achieving the team's mission, organizational objectives, and societal goals. Google introduced a structured method to measure individual and team performance.

ASSESSMENTS

1. Explain the key differences between a group and a team.
2. Please explain the various fundamentals of a team. Give suitable examples wherever required.
3. How will you develop a high-performance team within your organization?

CHAPTER 10

Building Organizational Culture

10.1 Organizational Culture and Its Significance

Organizational culture reflects an organization's personality. It comprises a standard set of accepted values, norms, and attitudes within the organization. This collective paradigm fosters a relatively uniform approach to interpreting the complexities encountered by the organization.

According to Schein, organizational culture refers to a pattern of fundamental assumptions that a group develops as it addresses its challenges of external adaptation and internal integration. These assumptions have been deemed effective enough to be regarded as valid. Thus, they are imparted to new members as the appropriate way to perceive, think, and feel regarding those challenges.

Over the past 40 years, organizational culture has become widely recognized as a valuable tool for understanding human systems. Increased competition in the global economy has heightened the need for a robust organizational culture. This culture can significantly impact an organization's long-term financial performance, either enhancing its ability to seize market opportunities or directly hindering it.

An organization's culture influences all employees' behavior; it guides their decision-making and shapes the fundamental way they conduct business. This hidden yet unifying force provides meaning and direction to the organization. It is learned, shared, and passed down from employee to employee over time, naturally emerging from people and systems.

Organizational culture is arguably the most critical factor influencing an organization's capacity, effectiveness, and longevity. It also significantly shapes the organization's brand image and promise. Employees are more likely to work for companies that provide unique experiences, take pride in their work, and value a distinctive work environment. Culture serves three important functions within organizations:

1. It creates a signature experience and the psychological energy required to achieve excellence.
2. Integrates members so they understand how to interact with one another.
3. Assists the organization in adapting to the external environment.

Culture shapes daily working relationships and influences how individuals communicate within the organization, what behaviors are deemed acceptable, and how power and status are distributed. It can instill a set of unwritten rules in employees' minds, significantly impacting their behavior and, in turn, organizational performance (Morgan, 1993). Culture connects employees, transforming the organization into a community rather than merely a group of isolated individuals.

Culture also influences how the organization achieves its goals and interacts with external stakeholders. The appropriate cultural values can enable the organization to respond effectively to customers' needs. Culture can foster employees' commitment to the organization's mission and goals.

Organizational culture generates energy and momentum. This energy permeates the organization, fostering new momentum for success. A high-performance organizational culture can help employees achieve excellence in collaborating within internal and external environments. It can transform available organizational resources into specific competencies and core competencies. While competitors can easily imitate organizational resources, competencies are extremely difficult to replicate.

10.2 Building Blocks of the Organizational Culture

Organizational culture can be understood as having two levels, as shown in Figure 10.1. The core level comprises psychological elements, including expressed values, norms, and attitudes. While these elements are not directly visible, they can be inferred from an organization's artifacts, the behaviors of its members, and the explanations and justifications for their actions.

On the surface, we find artifacts and phenomena that reflect these underlying psychological elements. These artifacts and phenomena include language, symbols, daily routines, resolutions, stories, and ceremonies.

Initially, when a new member joins the organization, they learn about the organizational values, behavioral norms, and attitudes, striving to remember these psychological elements and behave intentionally.

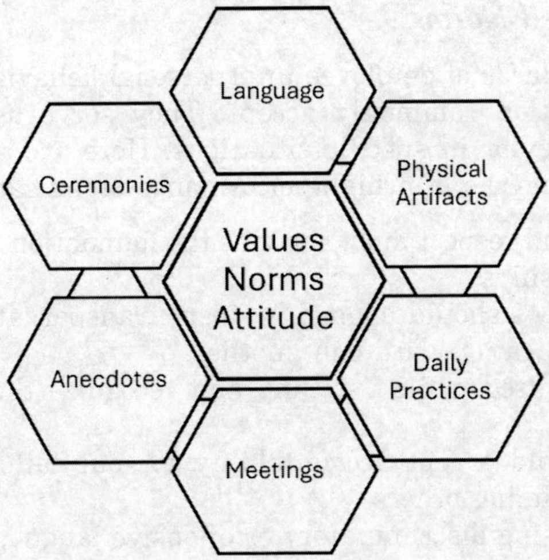

FIGURE 10.1 Cultural Web of the Organization.

For example, a new employee is aware that innovation is highly valued and rewarded in the company's culture. However, over time, these concepts become part of the employees' unconscious mindsets, making them less open to questioning. As a result, they may take innovation for granted. At this stage, innovation becomes an assumption, such as "employees are the source of innovation." Thus, various psychological elements and visible artifacts form the building blocks of the organization's culture.

To cultivate a high-performance organizational culture, merely calling a meeting and informing employees about expected behaviors will not suffice. Leaders must begin with the fundamental components of the organization.

1. *Widely Shared Organizational Values*

Organizational values are essential components for any organization, guiding employees in their behavior. These values can be divided into two distinct yet closely related types: terminal values and instrumental values.

Terminal values represent the desired outcomes that the organization aims to achieve. Examples of terminal values include excellence, responsibility, profitability, innovation, equality, and customer satisfaction.

The instrumental value represents the desired behaviors of employees, including open and honest communication, passion, having fun, being helpful and supportive, taking initiative, working hard, and being nimble and flexible.

Leaders must ensure that all employees emotionally align with organizational values and that their daily behaviors reflect both terminal and instrumental values.

2. *Widely Shared Norms*

Norms are standards of employee interpersonal behavior that members of the organization commonly accept. They serve as guidelines for appropriate behavior in specific situations. Here are some statements that reflect the norms of a high-performance organizational culture:

- Trust and respect must serve as the foundation of our workplace relationships.
- Employees should engage in open, transparent, and reciprocal communication with one another.
- Stay focused while listening and recognize the significance of diversity.
- We should accept accountability for our failures and refrain from blaming others.
- Avoid using discriminatory or offensive language and behavior.
- Encourage open communication and resolve conflicts in a constructive manner.

3. *Widely Shared Attitude*

In the context of organizational culture, attitude does not refer to personal preferences about a situation but rather to the actions taken to achieve the organization's vision and goals. Examples of shared attitudes in action include:

- **Make an impact on the universe:** We must make extraordinary efforts to transform the battleground in our industry. To change the battleground, organizations need to create exceptional value for people through their products, services, or innovations.
- **Jump the curve:** Rather than simply following the industry's growth curve, we must create a new, elevated performance curve defined by exceptional quality and revenue.
- **Work or does not work:** Something may work or may not work, but we should not be afraid to adopt new approaches and take bold leaps.
- **Refuse to accept anything less than the best:** We are not average individuals. We are extraordinary, giving our best and taking the best.
- **Zero Tolerance:** Discipline, excellent performance, and value-driven behavior should not be compromised.
- **Continuous Improvement:** No improvement is too small to overlook.

4. *Language*

Language plays a vital role in shaping organizational culture. It is an essential element that allows employees to express their thoughts, feelings, and information to one another. The language used in daily conversations reflects the organization's core values. Furthermore, the level of formality in communication provides insight into the organizational hierarchy and the mutual respect present in the workplace.

Clear and respectful language cultivates better understanding among employees. The types of words, jargon, acronyms, and phrases used in daily communication create a sense of belonging. Organizational values and norms are clearly reflected in policies, mission statements, and informal communications. The language used during discussions, feedback, or conflict resolution affects whether disagreements escalate or result in productive outcomes.

To foster positive language, leaders should encourage employees to use inclusive language, embrace transparent communication, reduce excessive jargon, and align their language with organizational values. This will promote transparency and trust within the organization.

5. *Physical Artifacts*

Physical artifacts serve as visual representations of organizational values. Examples include dress codes, logos, office decor, furnishings, the style of company vehicles, and hierarchical or horizontal organizational structures. These artifacts shape employees' behavior within the organization. For instance, employees tend to maintain a casual dress code in a relaxed and informal culture; however, they will adhere to a formal dress code in a culture that values professionalism.

Leaders who prioritize establishing a high-performance organizational culture are very mindful of the physical artifacts utilized within the organization. They understand that these artifacts represent more than mere objects; they reinforce organizational values, influence employee behavior, cultivate a sense of identity and belonging, and contribute to a productive work environment.

Leaders ensure office layouts foster efficient communication. Vision and mission statements are prominently displayed in common areas, and employees are expected to adhere to a professional dress code. Proper displays of trophies and records recognizing "Employee of the Month" should be maintained. Additionally, the use of ergonomic furniture, natural lighting, and appealing office aesthetics is encouraged. Branded merchandise, such as company t-shirts, mugs, and stationery, should also be utilized.

6. *Daily Practices*

Daily practices encompass the routine activities and behaviors that members of the organization engage in. These can be observed by examining what employees do each morning, throughout the day, and in the evening. How do they address problems and issues, and what procedures do they adopt to accomplish their tasks?

Stability in daily work enhances trust and reduces anxiety among employees. It establishes a structured environment where employees understand their tasks and what they can expect from the organization. This stability minimizes the time spent on decision-making and problem-solving, which in turn reduces burnout and increases job satisfaction. Effective time management also creates opportunities for brainstorming, fosters innovation, and encourages continuous improvement.

7. *Meetings*

Scheduled meetings at specific intervals create a routine that serves a meaningful purpose by bringing employees together. For instance, employees participate in a monthly sales review meeting, while board meetings are held quarterly.

Leaders ensure that meetings are productive and effectively address the agenda at regular intervals. Meetings held merely for the sake of meeting waste time; they should be structured appropriately to make decisions, resolve various issues, and promote continuous improvement.

Regular meetings serve as a powerful platform to reinforce the organization's mission and values, enhance employee morale, foster strong relationships, gather employee feedback, establish clear expectations, promote job security, retain top talent, integrate new hires, and boost overall employee engagement.

8. *Anecdotes*

Organizations often share the success stories of their heroes, illustrating the cultural values and norms within the organization. These stories provide valuable insights into the expected behaviors of employees. Organizations with numerous success stories cultivate pride among their employees and clearly define what it means to work there. For instance, a story about a salesperson who went above and beyond their normal job roles to satisfy customers can reinforce a culture of customer-first thinking. This is because employees relate more effectively to real-life examples, which inspire them to emulate such behavior. Therefore, anecdotes highlight the heroes' behaviors that lead to success and, in turn, establish standards for others to follow.

Many stories illustrate how organizations have overcome seemingly impossible challenges through resilience, adaptability, and innovation. These narratives offer valuable lessons for employees to navigate future challenges. To effectively utilize anecdotes in building a high-performance organizational culture, leaders should focus on collecting real-life stories and integrating them into meetings, training programs, ceremonies, artifacts, and everyday conversations.

9. *Ceremonies*

Organizations often host social events, such as annual functions, picnics, and birthday parties, to showcase their cultural values and norms to employees and stakeholders. Ceremonies play a crucial role in helping new hires integrate into the organization's culture and understand its values, norms, and attitudes. They enhance employee well-being throughout the organization. Leaders can utilize various ceremonies to motivate employees, foster a sense of security, enhance interpersonal relationships, and reinforce value-driven behavior among employees.

Southwest Airlines Culture

Southwest Airlines was founded by Herb Kelleher and Rollin King in 1966. It was initially named Air Southwest Co. but changed to Southwest Airlines in 1971. The airline aimed to be a low-fare, no-frills airline operating in various states across the USA. For nearly 45 years, Southwest Airlines has consistently been profitable, becoming one of the most successful airlines in the history of the aviation industry.

Herb Kelleher was a firm believer that if we treat employees right, they will treat our customers right. He was convinced that happy employees would naturally provide excellent customer service and go the extra mile in their performance. Consequently, he developed Southwest Airlines' culture around the core value of 'Employee First.' He established fun, humor, love, and a servant's heart as the guiding values of Southwest Airlines. Based on these values, the following practices were adopted by all Southwest employees.

- The company strongly emphasizes a fun-loving attitude when hiring employees, including pilots. During the hiring interview, applicants were encouraged to tell jokes, express individuality through singing, dancing, and sharing funny stories, and wear amusing clothing. Kelleher believed that individuals who can make jokes about themselves possess no ego while performing and wearing humorous clothing can be excellent team players. They are often willing to take on any job with enthusiasm. It was later observed that even pilots were assisting crew members in cleaning the aircraft for a quicker turnaround.
- Leaders at Southwest practice servant leadership, meaning they focus on serving their teams rather than commanding them. They possess servant's hearts and care for others with compassion. They do not take themselves too seriously.
- Front-level employees are empowered to participate in the company's strategic decision-making process.
- Managers at Southwest believe that there should be minimal meetings and a maximum focus on celebration.

Due to these practices, all the employees at Southwest developed resilience and became capable of dealing with any kind of problem without panicking. They achieved excellence in all their endeavors, making Southwest Airlines one of the most favored choices for professionals and business travelers in the USA.

10.3 High-Performance Culture

Organizational culture can be described in various ways. For clarity, we will define four distinct types of organizational cultures based on two key factors: performance levels (ranging from performance decline to productive performance) and leadership styles (which can be either positive or negative). The illustration in Figure 10.2 below depicts these four types of organizational culture.

- **Positive Leadership Style:** Positive leadership features participative decision-making, recognition, praise, rewards, and empowerment. This approach nurtures productive relationships among employees and between them and management, creating a sense of job security and enhancing employee well-being.
- **Negative Leadership Style:** In contrast, a negative leadership style is marked by dictatorship, autocratic decision-making, coercion, suspensions, terminations, and the threat of punishment. This leads to poor and fearful relationships among employees and between employees and management, leading to job insecurity, increased employee turnover, and a fearful work environment.
- **Performance Decline:** A decline in performance occurs when leaders focus too much on being people-oriented and strive for popularity among employees. In their effort to be liked by everyone, they avoid making tough decisions that could upset workers. As a result, underperformance often goes unaddressed, and employees resort to superficial kindness rather than addressing issues directly. Consequently, undeserving employees are rewarded simply to satisfy the leaders' egos.

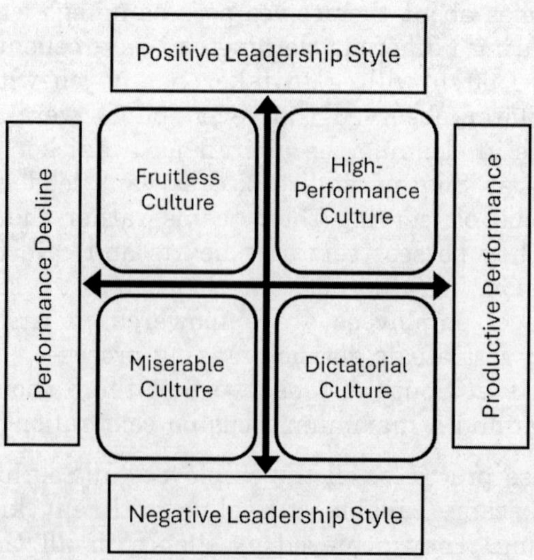

FIGURE 10.2 Types of Organizational Culture.

- **Productive Performance:** Productive performance occurs when leaders strike a balance between focusing on people and prioritizing performance. Leaders strive to be effective rather than merely pleasant. Their actions are guided by principles and a sense of what is right. The relationship between employees and management is transparent and objective, with direct addressing of underperformance. Rewards are given for authentic contributions, while those who face difficulties receive mentoring and counseling.
- **Fruitless Culture:** The fruitless culture is an unproductive culture, which is warm yet ineffective and marked by positive leadership styles alongside declining performance trends within the organization. While goals are mutually agreed upon, there are no real measures in place to achieve them. Employees lack accountability for meeting these goals. Although there is some communication among team members, it tends to be sporadic and ineffective, leading to wasted time on unproductive discussions. To keep subordinates unnecessarily happy, leaders often focus on pleasant conversations and share only positive news. As a result, employees engage in lip-service participation, characterized by plenty of talk but little action.

  Poor performances are often overlooked, with numerous excuses made for inadequate service and quality. There is no assessment of effectiveness in achieving goals or meeting service standards. Ineffective departments are not held accountable, leading to complacency among employees who prioritize maintaining harmony and avoiding conflict. Although everyone appears busy, they accomplish very little. They focus more on measuring activities rather than delivering tangible results.
- **Miserable Culture:** This type of culture reflects a negative leadership style characterized by strained relationships between managers and subordinates, often leading to declining organizational performance. The boss demands high performance without clearly communicating goals. A culture of secrecy prevails within the organization, and trust in the sharing of information is minimal. Communication among employees, as well as between managers and subordinates, is restricted. Consequently, many rumors tend to circulate within the workplace.

  Subordinates are not permitted to engage in the decision-making process. Managers tend to be coercive towards their team members, leading to the workforce being viewed as lazy. There is a deficiency of trust, and minimal responsibility is assigned to employees. Consequently, individuals often conceal poor quality, mistakes, or waste, and they frequently do not prioritize meeting standards.

Departments do not cooperate with one another and often blame each other for poor performance. Criticism occurs behind people's backs, creating a real fear of speaking openly. There is a great deal of focus on catching people doing things wrong.

- **Dictatorial Culture:** In this type of culture, a dictatorship exists within the organization. Despite the negative aspects of this leadership style, the overall organizational performance remains positive. This is primarily due to the fear instilled in employees by their dictatorial leaders. The boss sets goals without any consultation with employees, and communication is predominantly one-way, flowing from the top down. Managers occasionally allow their subordinates to participate in decision-making based on their individual needs. Leadership is often exercised through managers' status and position rather than through collaborative efforts.

  There are very few opportunities for subordinates to learn in this environment. Job boundaries are restrictive, and training for employees is limited. Workers tend to have the mindset that their boss knows best. Quality inspectors are responsible for ensuring compliance with standards, while quality control is typically viewed as a manager's responsibility. Employees rarely challenge their bosses' views or ideas and often fear doing so. Management enforces strict rules and constantly monitors employees.

- **High-Performance Culture:** In a high-performance organizational culture, there is a strong positive relationship among the people within the organization, fostered by an effective leadership style. Leaders engage in participative decision-making, mentoring, and counseling, as well as recognizing and rewarding genuine performance. They promote open communication and build trustful relationships.

  These relationships extend beyond mere work interactions, reaching deep into the hearts of the individuals involved, thereby creating mutual commitment to one another. As a result of this intense commitment, employees begin to care for each other, becoming compassionate and willing to take on each other's responsibilities. They also hold themselves accountable for each other's successes and failures.

  All employees are strongly aligned and emotionally committed to the organization's vision, mission, goals, and values. The organizational performance is positive and growing at the required pace. Employees effectively participate in the decision-making process, and goals are determined mutually. Effective measures are mutually developed to achieve the goals. Effective two-way communication prevails in the system. The organization maintains a democratic and open climate, ensuring transparency within its system.

People are empowered to make decisions and set their short-term goals. Self-directed teams monitor their performance and continuously strive for improvement. Everyone has the opportunity to contribute and is regarded as an expert in their own right. Quality and service are the responsibility of each individual performing the job. Ideas are shared openly, and everyone feels comfortable expressing differing opinions without fear of retaliation. All team members are focused on achieving results and delivering high-quality outputs.

People are innovative in their approach to achieving shared goals in their work. A high-performance organizational culture is inherently adaptive, with managers paying close attention to all stakeholders and fostering partnerships with them. Leadership is valued at every level; individuals are encouraged to take initiative and drive change when necessary to meet the legitimate interests of stakeholders. Leaders ensure that there is a culture of meritocracy so that rewards and promotions are based on actual performance rather than personal biases.

10.4 VRIO Framework

Barney and Wright (1998) discuss the VRIO framework, which stands for Value, Rarity, Inimitability, and Organization Exploitability. This framework is based on earlier literature, consulting activities, and input from executive training. It serves as a hierarchical guide for determining an organization's success through its internal resources. Barney and Wright developed this framework to evaluate the various internal resources that organizations use. In this course, we will specifically focus on applying this model to human resources. Figure 10.3 illustrates the VRIO framework as it pertains to human resources.

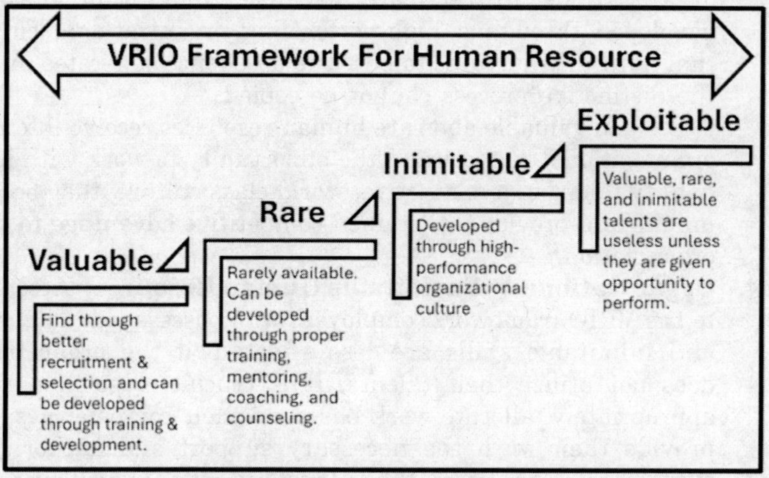

FIGURE 10.3 VRIO Framework.

1. **Valuable Human Resource:** The first level of the framework addresses whether our human resources are valuable. Organizations can either hire valuable resources from outside or transform ordinary resources into valuable assets through proper training and development. Non-valuable internal resources can result in a competitive disadvantage. In contrast, valuable human resources provide organizations with competitive parity.
2. **Rare Human Resource:** Rare human resource, as the name suggests, are individuals who are seldom found in the labor market. They possess exceptional talents, unique knowledge, skills, and competencies in their respective fields. These individuals demonstrate innovative thinking and strong leadership abilities, providing a competitive advantage to their companies.

   When individuals are recognized as valuable human resources and are provided with proper training, opportunities to perform, and guidance from their leaders, they can transform into exceptional and rare assets for the organization. This transformation can elevate the organization to the next level and offer a competitive advantage.
3. **Inimitable Human Resource:** While rare human resource provides a competitive advantage to organizations, this advantage is temporary. Over time, competitor organizations can also cultivate similar talents through comparable training and development.

   The highest level of achievement is reached when resources are valuable, rare, and difficult to imitate. Inimitable human resources are particularly challenging for competing organizations to replicate because their uniqueness is developed through a high-performing organizational culture that naturally nurtures talent. The excellence generated during the distinctive process cannot be copied.

   When valuable and rare human resources receive intensive organizational support and the opportunity to work with high-quality talent in a distinctive, world-class culture, they become unique and provide a sustained competitive advantage to their organization.
4. **Organizationally Exploitable Human Resource:** According to the VRIO framework, employees who possess valuable, rare, and inimitable skills are less effective if the organization does not utilize their talents. It is crucial to position them appropriately, allocate work based on their competencies, and provide them with the necessary support and authority to outperform competitors. When these exceptional employees are effectively utilized, the organization can achieve extraordinary performance.

ASSESSMENTS

1. Describe various building blocks of an organizational culture.
2. What are the four basic types of organizational cultures? Please provide examples where necessary.
3. Describe the VRIO framework related to human resources. How will you implement this framework in your organization?

Bibliography

Abraham F. Maslow, "A Theory of Human Motivation," Psychological Review, 50, 1943.

Andrew J. DuBrin, "Leadership: Research Findings, Practice, and Skills," Houghton Mifflin Company, Boston, 1995.

Bandura A., "Social Foundation of Thought and Action: A Social Cognitive Theory," Prentice-Hall (Englewood Cliffs, N. J.), 1986.

Cherie Carter-Scott, "Negaholics: How to Overcome Negativity and Turn Your Life Around," Random House Publishing Group, New York, 1999.

Csikszentmihalyi M., "Flow: The Psychology of Optimal Experience," Harper and Row, New York, 1990.

Dalai Lama, The Power of Compassion, Harper Collins, ISBN 9780007273959, 2007.

David C. McClelland, "The Two Faces of Power in Organizational Psychology," Prentice-Hall (Englewood Cliffs, N.J.), 1971.

David E. Bowen and Edward E. Lawler III, "Empowering Service Employees," Sloan Management Review (summer) 1995.

Donald Hambrick, David Nadler, Michael Tushman, "Navigating Change," McGraw-Hill, Sydney, 1997.

Edgar H. Schein, "Organizational Culture," American Psychologist 45, No. 2, February 1990.

Fred E. Fiedler, "The Efforts of Leadership Training and Experience: A Contingency Model Interpretation," Administrative Science Quarterly 17 (1972).

Frederick Herzberg, "One More Time: How Do You Motivate Employees?" Harvard Business Review, January-February, 1968.

Goleman, D., Emotional Intelligence: Why it can matter more than IQ, Bantam Books, 2005.

Grant. Cardone, The 10X Rule: The only difference between success and failure, John Wiley & Sons, ISBN 9781118064085, 2011.

Halifax J., Standing at the Edge: Finding Freedom Where Fear and Courage Meet, Flatiron Books, ISBN 978-1250101341, 2018.

Herminia Ibarra, "Networking is Vital for Successful Managers," Ambition: The Newsletter of Association of MBAs, Issue-8, October-December, London, 2008.

http://rescomp.stanford.edu/cheshire/Einstein_quotes.html

http://www.brainyquote.com/authers/m/mother_teresa.html

http://www.brainyquote.com/quotes/authers/m/mohandas_gandhi.html

http://www.viewonbudhhism.org/resources/buddhist_quotes.html

http://www.woopidoo.com/business_quotes/authors/mahatma-gandhi/index.htm

J. Stacy Adams, Inequity in Social Exchange, Advances in Experimental Social Psychology, Elsevier, Vol. 2, 1965.

James W. Robinson, Jack Welch, "Jack Welch and Leadership: Executive Lessons from the Master CEO," Forum Publishing, South Florida, 2001.

Jay B. Barney, Gaining and Sustaining Competitive Advantage (Third Edition), PHI Learning Private Limited, pages 138-151

John P. Kotter, "A Force of Change: How Leadership Differs from Management," Free Press (New York) 1990.

John P. Kotter, "Leading Change: Why Transformations Fail?" Harvard Business School Press, Boston, 1996.

John P. Kotter, "What Leaders Really Do," Harvard Business Review, May-June 1990.

John R. Katzenbach and Douglas K. Smith, "The Discipline of Teams," Harvard Business Review, March-April 1993.

John R. Katzenbach and Douglas K. Smith, "The Wisdom of Teams," Collins Business Essentials Edition 2006.

Joseph C. Rost, "Leadership for the Twenty-First Century" (Westport, CT: Praeger, 1993).

Khera S., "You Can Win," MACMILLAN India Limited, Delhi, 2002.

Kovach, Kenneth A., (1st ed) "Organization Size, Job Satisfaction, Absenteeism, and Turnover," University Press of America, N.H. 1978.

Lee, T.W., Locke, E.A., & Latham, G.P., Goal Setting Theory and Job Performance, L. A. Pervin, 1989.

Lieberman, M.D., Eisenberger, N.I., Crockett, M.J., Tom, S.M., Pfeiffer, J.H., and Way, B.M., "Putting Feelings Into Words: "Affect Labeling

Disrupts Amygdala Activity in Response to Affective Stimuli." Psychological Science, 18, No. 5, 2007.

Lipton, B., Biology of Belief: Unleashing the Power of Consciousness, Matter & Miracles, Hay House UK, ISBN 978-1401923129, 2011.

Luft, J. Ingham, H. (1955), "The Johari window, a graphic model of interpersonal awareness", Proceedings of the western training laboratory in group development, Los Angeles: University of California, Los Angeles, 1955.

Martin E. Nasser and F.J. Vivier, "Mindset for the New Generation Organization," Juta & Company Limited, South Africa, 1995.

Mehrabian A., "Silent Messages," Wadsworth, Belmont, California, 1971.

Missirian A.K. (Ed.), Reprinted in "The Case of Corporate Woman," Prentice-Hall, New York, 1981.

Nadler, R.S., Leading with Emotional Intelligence: Hands-on strategies for building confident and collaborative star performers, Tata McGraw-Hill, ISBN 978-0-07-107422-3, 2011.

Niels Bohr, Measurement Changes Everything. https://en.wikipedia.org /wiki/ Observer Effect_(physics).

Paul Hersey and Kenneth H. Blanchard, "Management of Organization Behavior: Utilizing Human Resources," 5th ed. (Englewood Cliffs, NJ: Prentice Hall, 1988).

Peter B. Scott Morgan, "Barriers to a High-Performance Business," Management Review, July 1993.

Peter F. Drucker, "Managing for the Future: The 1990s and Beyond" (New York: Truman Talley Books/Dutton, 1992).

Peter Koestenbaun, "Leadership: The Inner Side of Greatness," San Francisco: Jossey-Bass, 1991.

Peter Breyman., "What to Say When Your Employee Makes a Mistake," Harvard Business Review, 2019.

Prabhupada S., "Bhagavad–Gita As It Is," Shaktivedanta Book Trust, Mumbai, 2003.

Ralph M. Stogdill and Advin E. Coons (eds), "Leader Behavior: Its Description and Measurement," (Columbus, Ohio: The Ohio State University, Bureau of Business Research, 1957).

Ralph M. Stogdill, "Handbook of Leadership: A Survey of Theory and Research," Free Press (New York), 1971.

Robert E. Kelly, "The Power of Followership," New York: Doubleday, 1992.

Robert Hershey, "A practitioner's View of Motivation," *Journal of Managerial Psychology* (Vol. 8, Issue: 3), MCB UP Limited, 1993.

Robert J. House and Terence R. Mitchell, "Path-Goal Theory of Leadership," *Journal of Contemporary Business*, Autumn 1974.

Rotter, J.B. "Generalized Expectations of internal versus external control of reinforcements," Psychological Monographs – 80, Princeton 1996.

Ryan, R.M., Deci, E.L., Self-Determination Theory and Facilitation of Intrinsic Motivation, Social Development, and Well-Being. American Psychologist, 2000.

Ryuho Okawa, "Invincible Thinking: There is no such thing as a defeat," Jaico Publishing House, Mumbai, 2007.

Ryuzaburo Kaku, "The Path of Kyosei," Harvard Business Review, volume 75 (July-August 1997).

Schermerhorn John R. Jr., Richard N. Osborn, and James G. Hunt, "Core Concepts of Organizational Behavior," John Wiley & Sons, NJ, 2003.

Spreitzer M. Gretchen, "Psychological Empowerment in the Workplace: Dimensions, Measurement, Validation," Academy of Management Journal 38(5), San Francisco, 1995.

Stephen R. Covey, "The Seven Habits of Highly Effective People: Restoring the Character Ethic," G.K. Hall, 1997.

The Chemicals of Care: How Self-Compassion Manifests in Our Bodies. http://self-compassion.org/the-chemicals-of-care-how-self-compassion-manifests-in-our-bodies/

The Golden Sayings of Epictetus, edited by John Mark Ockerbloom (onlinebooks@pobox.upenn.edu).

The presence of Muons near Earth's surface is a good example of time dilation: http://hyperphysics.phy-astr.gsu.edu/hbase/Relativ/muon.html

This is My Story: An Autobiography of Eleanor Roosevelt, 1937.

Tolle. Eckhart, "Don't Let Your Ego Take Control of Your Life," Harvard Business Review, 2019.

Tony Blair, British Prime Minister, Press Conference, October 2000.

Victor E. Frankl, "Man's Search for Meaning," Washington Square Press, New York, 1984.

Victor H. Vroom and Arthur G. Jago, "The New Leadership: Managing Participation in Organizations," (Englewood Cliffs, NJ: Prentice Hall, 1988).

Warren Bennis and Burt Nanus, "The Leadership Tightrope," Success, March 1985.

William James, "The Will to Believe," Courier Dover Publications, New York, 1956.

William Rothschild, "Risk taker, Caretaker, Surgeon, Undertaker: The Four Faces of Strategic Leadership" (New York: John Wiley, 1993).

Index